BIRDS OF A FEATHER
SAVING RARE TURKEYS
FROM EXTINCTION

Carolyn J. Christman

Robert O. Hawes

THE AMERICAN LIVESTOCK BREEDS CONSERVANCY

Pittsboro, North Carolina

The American Livestock Breeds Conservancy
PO Box 477, Pittsboro, NC 27312 USA

Birds of a Feather: Saving Rare Turkeys from Extinction

© 1999 by the American Livestock Breeds Conservancy
All rights reserved. Published 1999.
Printed in the United States by Glover Printing, Inc., Raleigh, NC
First printing 1999

The information presented in this book is true and complete to the best of our knowledge. The authors and publisher disclaim any liability in connection with the use of this information.

Carolyn J. Christman 1957-
Birds of a Feather: Saving Rare Turkeys from Extinction /
by Carolyn J. Christman and Robert O. Hawes
Includes index

ISBN 1-887316-03-5

Cover: Bronze turkey. Drawing by Meg Kratz, © ALBC.
Back cover: Wishard Bronze turkeys at sunset. Photo by David Sullenberger.

Acknowledgements

The writing and production of this book have been supported by the Barkley Fund, the C. S. Fund, the Charles DeVlieg Foundation, the Geraldine R. Dodge Foundation, the Kind World Foundation, and the Mary D. B. T. Semans Foundation. Members of the American Livestock Breeds Conservancy have also provided financial support. We are especially grateful to Nan Crocker, Scott and Jill Crocker, Mary Gano, Robert Johnson, Ann Lennartz, Russell Mawby, Robyn and Robert Metcalfe, and Robert and Bonnie Prots.

Many people have contributed to our knowledge about turkeys, but a few merit special acknowledgement. R. D. Crawford was the first to call for poultry genetic conservation in North America and around the world; his work laid a foundation for what ALBC has been able to accomplish. Donald Bixby and Phillip Sponenberg of ALBC provide the technical focus for ALBC's conservation strategies today and made significant additions to the book. Ed Buss, retired from Pennsylvania State University, and Tom Savage of Oregon State University provided help in the identification and explanation of color patterns. *Turkey World* magazine was our best source of information on the history of the turkey industry. Glenn and Linda Drowns, Paula Johnson, Frank Reese, and Craig Russell provided information on the status and prospects of rare varieties. Frank Reese also contributed his story for this book.

Birds of a Feather would not have been possible without the images contributed by talented photographers and artists. We are especially grateful to Phillip Sponenberg, whose photographs describe the rare varieties, and to Frank Fretz, who made original drawings for the book. *Turkey World* magazine granted use of several historic photographs, and Polly Schaafsma loaned historic images of turkeys in the Southwest. Deborah Wechsler designed the book, and Marjorie Bender, Donald Bixby, Cynthia Ehrman, Mary Ellen Nicholas, and Deborah Wechsler did much to polish its text.

We dedicate this book to the people who are stewards of turkey genetic diversity. May their work be successful in protecting these unique "birds of a feather" from extinction.

Turkeys

One November
a week before Thanksgiving
the Ohio River froze
and my great uncles
put on their coats
and drove the turkeys
across the ice
to Rosiclare
where they sold them
for enough to buy
my grandmother
a Christmas doll
with blue china eyes

I like to think
of the sound of
two hundred turkey feet
running across to Illinois
on their way
to the platter,
the scrape of their nails
and my great uncles
in their homespun leggings
calling out gee and haw and git
to them as if they
were mules

I like to think of the Ohio
at that moment,
the clear cold sky
the green river sleeping
under the ice,
before the land got stripped
and the farm got sold
and the water turned the color
of whiskey
and all the uncles
lay down
and never got up again

I like to think of the world
before some genius invented
turkeys with pop-up plastic
thermometers
in their breasts,
idiot birds
with no wildness left in them,
turkeys that couldn't run the river
to save their souls

—Mary Mackey

White Holland turkeys. Drawing by F. L. Sewell.

Table of Contents

Introduction

THE TURKEY SPECIES brings three very different images to mind. Wild turkeys are alert, intelligent and imposing birds, a challenge for the bird watcher and the hunter alike. Almost extinct a few decades ago, these turkeys now number in the millions. In contrast, domestic turkeys are docile, colorful, and gregarious. They were historically found in several distinct types and varieties, which made the turkey species valuable to farmers in many cultures and over several centuries. The third image of turkeys comes from the highly specialized and productive industrial stocks which are an integral part of today's food supply. These birds demonstrate the great accomplishments of modern breeding technologies and the potential Achilles' heel of genetic uniformity.

This book is concerned primarily with the historic varieties of domestic turkeys. Almost all of these varieties are critically rare today, and many are near extinction. At the same time, they represent the genetic diversity necessary to protect the biological health of the turkey species and its usefulness in agriculture. Our goal is to introduce readers to the beauty and value of turkeys and tell the fascinating

Glenn Drowns is pictured holding a Narragansett turkey. Photo by Phillip Sponenberg.

1

story of turkey husbandry for the past 2,000 years. We hope to inspire you to join this unique conservation project, either by raising rare varieties or buying rare turkey products from breeders and farmers. It is only through the efforts of many people all across North America that the complete legacy of turkey diversity – nurtured for centuries – will survive for the next generation.

Chapter 1

A Natural History of the Turkey

"... Others object to the Bald Eagle as looking too much like a Turkey. For my own part, I wish the Bald Eagle had not been chosen as the Representative of our Country; he is a Bird of bad moral Character. For in truth, the Turkey is in comparison a much more respectable Bird, and withal a true original Native of America. Eagles have been found in all Countries, but the Turkey was peculiar to ours ... He is, though a little vain and silly, it is true, but not the worse emblem for that, a Bird of Courage, and would not hesitate to attack a Grenadier of the British Guards, who should presume to invade his Farmyard with a red coat on."

— Benjamin Franklin, in a letter to his daughter Sarah Bache,
January 26, 1784, cited by Richard Powell (1990)

THE TURKEY IS ONE of the few domesticated animals native to the Americas. It likely evolved from pheasant-like ancestors in North America or Asia during the Pleistocene Era, between 15,000 and 50,000 years ago (Crawford 1984). Two species of turkeys are known: *Meleagris gallopavo* of North America and *Meleagris ocellata* of Central America.

Wild turkeys

The North American wild turkey (*M. gallopavo*) is divided into six subspecies. The subspecies have been named and defined by their geographic ranges and by their characteristics. At the same time, the current genetic status and relationship of these sub-species is not clear. Breeding among them occurs in areas where their ranges overlap and has also resulted from captive propagation and reintroduction of wild turkeys (Crawford 1984). Most wild turkey populations east of the Mississippi have also had some introductions of genetic material from the domestic strains (Schorger 1966).

The most numerous and widely distributed of the subspecies is the Eastern wild turkey (*M. g. silvestris*), which is native to the eastern half of the United States. "Silvestris" translates as "forest turkey," and this describes its habitat. The National Wild Turkey Federation estimates that there may be as many as three million Eastern wild turkeys alive today, perhaps three-quarters of the total wild turkey population of the United States (Kennamer and Kennamer n.d.).

The Rio Grande wild turkey (*M.g. intermedia*) is native to the open lands of the central and southern Plains. Now found in a range from South Dakota to Texas, this subspecies is the second most numerous. Its taxonomic name was apparently suggested by characteristics intermediate between the turkeys of the United States and the turkeys of Mexico.

Merriam's wild turkey (*M.g. merriami*) is native to the ponderosa pine and juniper woodlands and mountains of the southwestern United States from Colorado to Mexico. This habitat, much of it between 6,000 and 10,000 feet in elevation, has given this subspecies the common name "mountain turkey." Merriam's turkeys were domesticated by the Pueblo and other peoples of the Southwest by 700 AD, and both wild and domestic birds have been important in Pueblo mythology and religion since that time (Tyler 1979). This subspecies almost became extinct earlier this century but today it is the third most numerous. The Merriam's turkey was named for C. Hart Merriam, first chief of the U.S. Biological Survey.

The Florida wild turkey (*M.g. osceola*) is found on the peninsula of Florida and is named after the famous Seminole chief. It is similar to the Eastern turkey but smaller and darker. This subspecies, with an estimated population of about 80,000, is the fourth most numerous.

A fifth subspecies, the Gould's turkey (*M.g. mexicana*), is known in the southwestern United States and northern Mexico. It was described by J. Gould, who traveled to Mexico in 1856. This subspecies is not well understood. The National Wild Turkey Federation has projects underway to study the Gould's turkey, increase its population, and expand its range in the United States (Kennamer and Kennamer n.d.).

The sixth subspecies (*M.g. gallopavo*), or Mexican turkey, was historically found in southern Mexico, with a range between Puerta Vallarta and Acapulco on the Pacific coast and Vera Cruz and Tuxpan on the Gulf of Mexico (Mallia 1998). Turkeys were domesticated in this region about 2,000 years ago. Today, however, this Mexican subspecies is quite rare, both in its wild form and as descendant domestic strains, and evaluation of the remaining stocks is urgently needed (National Research Council 1991). Fortunately, the first steps of such work are now underway. Recent research by J. G. Mallia (1998) on turkeys in the Mexican states of Oaxaca and Quintana Roo found that indigenous domestic turkey populations, though endangered, do survive in many areas. They are known as *pavo* (the traditional Spanish word for turkeys) or as *pavo creollo* to distinguish them from the improved, imported types. These turkeys inspire a sense of pride and are valued for their historic role in the local cultures and the delicious flavor of their meat. According to Mallia, their prospects for survival seem promising, especially in Oaxaca, if conservation efforts can be initiated. Such a conservation effort would benefit the turkey species

Eastern wild turkeys are alert and imposing in appearance. Photo © Tom Evans Outdoor Stock Photos.

and the people of the region.

The same taxonomic classification (*M.g. gallopavo*) also includes all varieties of improved domesticated turkeys.

Central American turkeys are classified as a different species, *Meleagris ocellata*, also known as the Ocellated turkey. (*Agriocharis ocellata* was the previous classification.) This species is found in Belize, Honduras, and the Yucatan. The name "ocellated," from the Latin word *oculus* for eye, describes the round, eye-like color patterns on its feathers. These patterns, plus a brilliant blue and green color, have given the species the name "peacock turkey." Ocellated turkeys are smaller than North American turkeys and make distinctive drumming sounds and high-pitched gobbles. These turkeys may well have been domesti-

The Ocellated Turkey is a stunningly beautiful wild species of Central America. (Series 1, Plate 1) © Thomas A. Bennett.

cated by the Mayans, whose ruins often include appropriately-sized stone pens with elevated soil levels of phosphorous and potassium. Even today in the rural Peten region of Guatemala, Ocellated turkeys are sometimes found as scavengers around houses (National Research Council 1991), though the overall population of the species is declining rapidly due to loss of habitat, pressure from predators, and over-hunting. It is in urgent need of conservation (Taylor, Quigley, and Gonzalez n.d.).

The status of wild turkeys

Wild turkeys were very common in North America when European colonists first arrived in the early 1600s. After only a few decades of colonization, however, land clearing began to reduce turkey habitat. By the early 1800s, wild turkeys had disappeared from much of New England. A century later, they had also been lost from Ontario and from the Midwestern states. In the 1930s, wild turkeys survived in only the most inaccessible places. It was not until federal efforts to restore wildlife habitat began after World War II that wild turkey populations began to increase in the United States.

The initial strategy taken to expand wild turkey populations was to propagate them as domestic stocks and then release them into the wild. The release of domestic-raised "wild" turkeys was, however, a resounding failure. By the 1970s, the reason was clear: these young birds did not survive in the wild because they lacked the survival behaviors that wild-born turkeys learned from their mothers in the first months of life. It was also realized that in addition to being ineffective, the release program had introduced diseases to wild populations. Today, release of domestic-raised wild turkeys is strongly discouraged if not illegal in most states.

Instead, successful re-establishment of wild turkey populations was based on the re-location of existing wild flocks to new locations. The development of cannon-net and drop-net techniques, as well as improvements in immobilizing drugs for turkeys eventually allowed for the safe capture and relocation of a large number of birds. The National Wild Turkey Federation estimates that wild turkey populations have increased from fewer than 500,000 in 1959 to over four million in 1994. Turkeys are now found in all states except Alaska (Kennemer, Kennemer, and Brenneman n.d.).

The characteristics of turkeys

Turkeys are large and impressive birds, standing as tall as four feet with a wing span of nearly six feet. The courting behavior of the male turkey, in which he struts and displays his wing and tail feathers, is a distinguishing characteristic of the species (Crawford 1984).

When people have a chance to see turkeys close up, they are often amazed by the birds' unusual appearance. The head and neck of the turkey are bare of feathers, covered instead by wrinkled or carunculated skin. The skin color is generally red but changes readily from red to dark blue to bluish white. A fleshy "snood" (or "frontal caruncle") attaches above the beak and hangs down beside the beak. The snood is found in both sexes but it is more prominent in males. A single "wattle" is attached from below the beak down the throat. Male turkeys (and occasionally females) have a long hair-like appendage on the breast known as a "beard." The beard is composed of primitive contour feathers which are not molted and can attain a length of twelve inches in old males. Male turkeys are called toms, cocks, or gobblers, and females are called hens. Young turkeys are called poults.

Turkeys are exquisitely adapted to life in the wild. As Watson (1912) describes, "Wild turkeys form an excellent illustration of the survival of the fittest... [their] slender, alert appearance is striking. The breadth of shoulders, deep chest, and firm step are noticeable. The head has a clean, game-like appearance, and the eyes are full of intelligence and suspicion." Turkeys cover a large range, and they eat a variety of foods, including seeds, nuts, fruit,

Wild turkeys thrive in a wide variety of conditions and climates. Photo by Julie DeVlieg.

insects, and plants. The wild turkey hen has extraordinary maternal abilities, and, after hatching her poults, she spends four to six months raising them.

While turkeys thrive in a wide range of environments and climatic conditions, they also have characteristics that make them well suited for domestication: they are flock-oriented rather than solitary; they lack a strong pair-bond and can thus be kept with fewer males than females; they may tolerate close proximity to people in order to explore new sources of food; and they can be fed a diet consisting almost entirely of plant material plus insects they find on their own.

Domestication of turkeys first occurred about 2,000 years ago, and selection by humans has changed the turkey in several ways. Conformation has been gradually transformed from the slim, long-legged and athletic appearance of the wild turkey to a domestic bird that is heavier with a more rounded breast and shorter legs. Tractability has been nurtured at the expense of alertness and cunning. Domestic turkeys are generally friendly and docile. (The exception may be toms during mating season.)

Color variety has been emphasized; this has been a priority for breeders since the time of the Aztecs. Wild turkeys generally show a single basic color pattern, though there are differences between the subspecies in the degree or bronzing over the back and in the color of the terminal band on the main tail feathers and coverts. Color mutations are occasionally found in wild flocks, including red, black, albino, and the striking Narragansett pattern, though these do not seem to be maintained under natural conditions. Color oddities occur in all subspecies but are most common in the Eastern subspecies (Kennamer 1995). The

This Bronze turkey close-up shows the carrunculated skin of a turkey's head. Photo by David Sullenberger.

domestic varieties carry a beautiful array of colors based on black, brown, red, and white in several different patterns; some of these mutations were known in the Mexican subspecies.

Domesticated turkeys have also been selected for production qualities, such as larger body size, more rapid growth rate, earlier maturity, and greater egg production. For example, wild hens lay ten to twelve eggs per nest, with one nest per year. If the hen's nest is disturbed, she will renest once or twice, but she only lays the eggs that she can hatch and produces the poults she can raise. In contrast, domesticated turkeys lay 30–90 eggs per year, depending on the variety and the management system. For example, exhibition stocks which are given no extra light stimulation will lay 30–40 eggs their first season, while intensively managed industrial strains should produce 85–95 eggs in their first laying season.

A comparison of sizes between different types of turkeys is another way to see how the species has changed. Wild turkey toms weigh 10–15 pounds and hens 7–10 pounds at one year old. Mature toms may weigh over 20 pounds. When domestic turkey varieties were first recognized by the American Poultry Association in 1874, the standard weights demonstrated the larger weights of these birds: White Holland 26 pounds (toms) and 16 pounds (hens); Slate and Buff 27 pounds (toms) and 18 pounds (hens); Narragansett 32 pound (toms) and 22 pounds (hens); and Bronze 35 pounds (toms) and 20 pounds (hens). These varieties were a great improvement over the narrow-breasted conformation of wild turkeys, but the rate of growth was not changed appreciably. By these historic standards, birds were not considered mature until 18 months old.

Today, the turkey industry looks for a market hen to reach 15–19 pounds at 13–16 weeks of age. Hens from the female breeder line, to be used for reproduction, will weigh 23–25 pounds at maturity and should produce at least 90 eggs in a 24 week production cycle; the eggs in turn should yield at least 68 poults. Market males should reach 30–44 pounds within 17–23 weeks. Toms from the male breeding line, which provide the growth element to the breeding package, can reach 65 pounds or more by the end of the breeding period. The cost of such intense selection has been the loss of the ability to mate naturally, a trait no longer found in industrialized turkeys due to the conformation and size of these huge males.

According to Roy Crawford (1984), the past 40 years of selection have done more to transform the domestic turkey than all the selection in previous centuries. Industrial turkeys are far more productive than the historic domestic varieties by almost any measure of performance. The rare varieties, however, retain the adaptability and survival characteristics necessary to thrive out of doors, forage for much of their own food, raise their own young, and provide pest control for diversified farms. These turkeys are an important genetic complement to the industrial stocks as well as to the wild relatives they have in common.

Large White turkeys have been selected for production characteristics such as body size and growth rate. Photo by USDA-APHIS.

"The Domestic Turkey" from The Poultry Book, *by John C. Bennett (1850).*

What does "turkey" mean?

The origin of the word "turkey" is a mystery. The Aztecs called turkeys *huerolotl,* while the Spanish words were *pavos, gallopavos,* or *guajolotes,* from Latin for peacock. The Italian term for turkeys was *galli d'India* (birds of the Indies), and the French used *dindes* or *dindon.* The Hebrew word for big bird or peacock was *tukki,* and this may have been used by Hebrew poultry merchants in Spain and England. Turkey may also have been inspired by the birds' call notes "turk, turk, turk" (Jull 1930).

Some writers have speculated that the name turkey comes from the European practice in the 1500s of naming exotic curiosities, including those from the New World, according to associations with the ancient kingdoms of the Orient, including "Turkii." It is possible that turkeys got their name from being originally called "turkey fowl" (McGinty 1978). Linneas' taxonomic name for turkey, *Meleagris gallopavo,* proposed in 1758, reflects the confusion of the times, combining *Meleagris,* the term for guinea fowl, with *gallopavo,* including *gallus* for chicken and *pavo* for peafowl.

Turkey Feathers

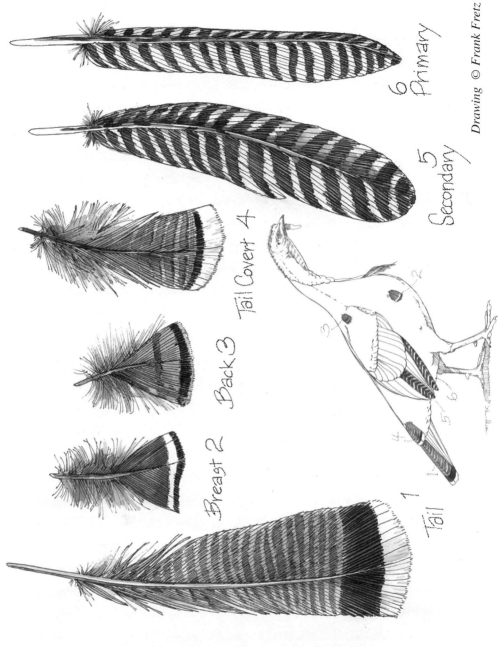

(Narragansett variety is pictured)

Axial feather – the short feather in the middle of each wing that separates the primary and secondary feathers

Contour feathers – all of the soft body feathers except the filoplumes and the large stiff feathers of the wings and tail. Turkeys may have 4,000 to 5,000 or more of these feathers.

Coverts – the feathers covering the base of the main tail feathers or the base of the large wing feathers.

Filoplumes – hair-like feathers next to the skin

Primaries – the large, outer feathers of the wing. There are usually ten primaries on each wing.

Fluff – soft, fluffy feathers near the vent or, more generally, the fluffy part of the feathers

Main tail feathers – large, stiff feathers of the tail. Turkeys normally have 18 main tail feathers, each 13–15 inches long.

Pinion feathers – the small group of short, stiff feathers attached to the last joint of the wing

Quill – hollow lower portion of the stem of a feather

Secondaries – large feathers of the wing located between the axial feather and the body. Each wing has 18–20 secondaries.

Adapted from Marsden and Martin (1939)

Tail 1

Breast 2

Back 3

Tail Covert 4

Secondary 5

6 Primary

Drawing © Frank Fretz

10

Turkey Conformation

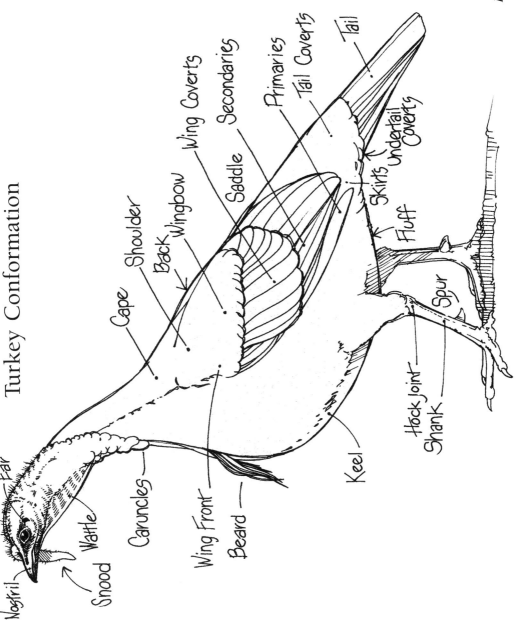

Nostril
Ear
Snood
Wattle
Caruncles
Cape
Shoulder
Back
Wingbow
Wing Coverts
Secondaries
Saddle
Primaries
Tail Coverts
Tail
Undertail Coverts
Skirts
Fluff
Wing Front
Beard
Keel
Hock Joint
Shank
Spur

Chapter 2

Turkeys in Agriculture and Industry

"With its size, majestic appearance, its marvelous beauty of plumage, and the most savory character of its flesh, the turkey may justly be termed the king of domestic fowls. Moreover, on account of its place of origin and because it is the only native fowl of this country which has taken an important place among domesticated poultry, it is a bird in which Americans can feel a special pride and pleasure."

—Harry M. Lamon and Rob R. Slocum (1924)

TURKEYS WERE FIRST DOMESTICATED by the Aztecs in south central Mexico about 2,000 years ago. The date is suggested by archaeological sites such as Tehuacan (200 BC–700 AD). Gary Nabhan (1989) speculates that domestication occurred in areas where human populations were increasing and required a more reliable source of meat than could be provided through hunting.

Domestic turkeys were also valued for their variety of feather colors, and they were selectively bred for color, including red, brown, black, and white. Feathers were made into mantles, robes, and blankets. Turkeys were extensively traded throughout the region along with other native birds, including partridge, quail, macaws, and wild ducks. Both live turkeys and cooked meat were offered in the marketplace (Schorger 1966).

The Pueblo people of the southwestern United States also domesticated turkeys (*M. g. merriami*) in approximately 600–700 AD. Turkeys appear in numerous prehistoric pictographs, including those in Anasazi and historic Navajo and Hopi settlements, and were the most commonly represented bird life in canyon country rock art (Nabhan 1989). They had practical value: turkey feathers were woven into garments and quilts, their meat was an important food source, and their bones could be made into tools and musical instruments. Of these, the use of feathers was the most important and may have been the primary reason that turkeys were domesticated. Compared to wild birds, domesticated turkeys were an easy source of large quantities of feathers!

The turkey was even more important for its place in Pueblo beliefs. Tyler (1979) describes this role extensively. For the Pueblo people, the turkey "represents the Earth as fittingly as the eagle represents the sky … Being of and on the Earth, turkeys also became man's companion, both in life and in death." Turkey feathers were used on prayer sticks to accompany the offering; they are often referred to as the "clothes" of the offerings, keeping them warm as the feather garments kept the people warm. Turkey feathers are also used alone as messages of serious importance – appeasement, direction, or need. In the Zuni culture, "turkeys

*These turkey petroglyphs were found at the Southern Tewa, Galisteo Basin,
New Mexico, and dated approximately 1325–1525. Photo © Polly Schaafsma.*

are called *wotsanna* or 'little servant' because they are so important in communicating with the spirits" (Tyler 1979). Turkeys also were believed to represent the dead. Their feathers were wrapped around human corpses and were worn by the spiritual representatives of the dead.

When Cortez and other Spanish explorers reached Central America and Mexico in the early 1500s, they found large numbers of both wild and domesticated turkeys. The Aztec ruler Montezuma kept flocks of black, brown, red, and white turkeys in his aviary in Mexico City (McGinty 1978). Explorers described turkeys in accounts of their journeys and received them as gifts wherever they went (Mallia 1998, Schorger 1966). Accounts describe the similarities between turkeys and peacocks – the size, plumage color, and display – but also the differences, such as the skin of the head and the better flavor of the meat.

Turkeys were first taken back to Spain between 1500 and 1519. They were present in Italy by 1520, France by 1538, England by 1541, and soon afterwards were found across Europe. The rapidity of the spread of turkeys and the diversity described suggests that several shipments of turkeys were made. Turkey was served at wedding and holiday feasts by the middle of the sixteenth century, and recipes for turkey were published by 1570 by Bartholomeo Scappi, the chef to Pope Pius V. Commentaries about turkey colors also appear before 1600 (McGinty 1978), and turkeys were found on English coats of arms and crests by about this time (Johnson 1998). The turkey, an American treasure, had become an international phenomenon in less then a century.

Turkey raising in North America

The turkey completed its trans-Atlantic round trip when colonists coming to Jamestown brought turkeys along. When that enterprise came to its unfortunate end, any remaining turkeys presumably escaped; this was the first of many instances where "domestic" genes were introduced into Eastern wild turkey populations. Turkeys were taken to Massachusetts by 1629 and to the other colonies afterwards. By 1700, they were plentiful in the mid-Atlantic region and throughout the coastal South, being noted in Biloxi, Mississippi, by 1699 (Schorger 1966).

Among the turkeys brought at various

times were the White Holland, the Norfolk Black, and the Spanish Black. These European strains of domesticated turkeys were smaller than the Eastern wild turkeys that colonists encountered, and the crossing of these two populations resulted in larger and more vigorous turkey stocks. De Crevecoeur describes this practice in *Letters from an American Farmer*, his account of rural life in the 1780s. He writes, "… the great secret consists in procuring the eggs of the wild sort and then [in crossing] that breed. In that case, we are always sure of a hardier and heavier bird. I have often killed them that weighed 27 pounds." At the same time, this practice was not always successful. It was not uncommon for hybrid turkeys to revert to the wild (Schorger 1966).

Turkey use in the colonies was marked by a new role, that of pest control. Tobacco was the primary cash crop of the Chesapeake region, but its production was always imperiled by the tobacco hornworm, the larva of a type of sphinx moth. Tobacco worms could be hand-picked off the plants by people, but turkeys were a better choice. "The main use of turkeys in this period (1750–1830) and perhaps later was their effectiveness in removing insect pests from cultivated tobacco. This function has been so thoroughly supplanted by chemical controls that the turkey's contribution to one of the most important agricultural products of the region is now wholly forgotten" (Powell 1990).

J. F. D. Smyth, author of *Tour of the United States*, made these comments in 1784: "As it would be endless labor to keep their hands constantly in search of them (tobacco hornworms), it

would be almost impossible to prevent their devouring more than half the crop had it not been discovered that turkeys are particularly dexterous at finding them, eat them up voraciously, and prefer them to every other food. For this purpose, every planter keeps a flock of turkeys, which he has driven into the tobacco grounds every day" (Powell 1990). George Washington and Thomas Jefferson also write about turkeys for pest control, and references even appear in James Fenimore Cooper's novel *The Spy* (1821), when one character, referring to another as a "voracious beast of prey," says, "If I had you on a Virginia plantation for a quarter of an hour, I'd teach you to worm tobacco with the turkeys" (Powell 1990). After harvest, turkeys would be penned and fattened for the holidays.

According to folklore, wild turkey was served as the main course at the first Thanksgiving celebration at Plymouth Colony. This may or may not be true, but the turkey has long been associated with our day of feasting. The link between Thanksgiving and the turkey

Until this century, most farms kept small flocks of turkeys for home use and seasonal income. This photo of James Austin feeding turkeys on his farm in Lorain County, Ohio is from a homemade calendar dated 1905, courtesy of his great-great-niece, Alice Hawes.

This historic site interprets the year 1895 in Oklahoma and keeps a flock of Bronze turkeys among its livestock. Photo courtesy of Jim Combs.

has played a major role in promoting the breeding and marketing of turkeys. The timing of the holiday (after harvest) fit the pest-control use of turkeys perfectly.

Cookbooks of the colonial period have recipes for turkey, including directions on how to select, stuff, roast, and carve birds. As one English traveler wrote in the 1780s, "At dinner, there are frequently four or five turkies on the table … I will mention that I do not recollect to have dined a single day from my arrival in America, til I left Virginia, without a turkey on the table" (Schorger 1966). Turkey feathers also had value for fans, dusters, and garments, and the quills were used for ink pens.

During the 1800s, most farmers kept small flocks of turkeys as a seasonal crop and for home use. The birds could be raised economically by feeding them vegetables and other farm produce, including beets, cabbage, potatoes, and turnips, as well as giving them an opportunity to forage. "Where range can be given, the turkey will find large quantities of insects, such as grasshoppers, and great quan-

tities of green vegetation, berries and wild grapes, weed seeds, waste grain, nuts, and acorns of various kinds, which they eat readily and which make the cost of raising them very small and the profits large" (Lamon and Slocum 1924). Range rearing was preferred over confinement due to the fact that turkeys suffered from reduced health and vigor when kept closely together and not given exercise (Watson 1912).

The more specialized production of turkeys was also beginning. Susan Swaysgood, author of *California Poultry Practice* (1915) described raising turkeys this way: "The foothills of California are the turkeys' paradise. In most localities they can roam the hills, picking up acorns that drop from the oak trees, fruit from wild vines and seeds and the insect life that is a part of such growth. For the rancher with a few acres of land, there is not anything that will pay a better dividend than a good flock of Bronze turkeys."

The role of turkeys in pest control continued to be important, though by the early

1900s, it was apparently less common than before. "The great value of these birds as insect destroyers is often overlooked. Much is said about the damage they do to growing crops and nothing about the good. As a matter of fact, turkeys do little damage to crops under ordinary conditions where they can find an amply supply of the feed which they love to glean in their own way. But the loss which they prevent by the destruction of insects is often very considerable. Recently attention was called to the fact that in one farming community the only farmer who was successful in securing a yield of clover seed was one who had allowed a flock of turkeys to range in his clover field. In the same locality, another farmer had his oat crop saved from grasshoppers by turning in a flock of turkeys to prey on them. A brood of turkeys when ranging through a field seeking their feed go about their work in a very systematic manner, often advancing in a line at distances apart just about great enough to enable them to cover all of the ground between one another as they advance. Not many grasshoppers get by this advancing line" (Lamon and Slocum 1924).

Farmers usually sold their turkeys live, and in many parts of the country the easiest way to get the birds to market was to drive them. These drives were sometimes called "turkey trots." In Texas, for example, 30 men could drive a flock of 8,000 turkeys thirteen miles to market in two days. A wagon would go in front of the turkeys, throwing out corn to keep the leaders going the right direction (Lamon and Slocum 1924). Many drives were much longer and more ambitious, such as one described by Johnson (1998a) in which turkeys were driven from California over the Sierra mountains to Carson City, Nevada. Schorger (1966) quotes an interesting first person account of turkey driving east of Denver, Colorado, in 1863. "We were much interested in a man who had a large drove of over 500 turkeys driven by two boys. The owner had bought them in Iowa and Missouri. His wagon, drawn by six horses and mules, was loaded with shelled corn. The birds also foraged on grasshoppers. At night they roosted all over his wagon, and many of them lay limp in the sand. At early dawn, they were all up chasing the first grasshopper. When the wind was favorable, the boys had an easy time

The eighth All-American Turkey Show held in Grand Forks, North Dakota, in 1931. Photo courtesy of Turkey World *magazine.*

17

driving them, and they could make as much as 25 miles in a day. But when the wind was from the west, you may be sure the two boys had their hands full. They wore out a good many pairs of moccasins on that trip." Other accounts describe less successful drives where the turkeys escaped and were not recovered.

In the early 1900s, about six million turkeys were being produced annually. Prices ranged between twelve and twenty cents per pound, up to forty cents per pound at the holiday season, and the demand was not met. Since the cost of production was about eight cents per pound, "no meat was produced for higher profit," according to Harrison Weir (1909). This economic potential led to specialization of the turkey industry and the growth of a national turkey market which would soon overshadow local and regional markets.

The growth of the national market was reflected in the initiation of turkey shows. The selling of poults was an important source of income for breeders, and shows were an excellent means of promotion. In 1924, the first "All-American Turkey Show" was held in Grand Forks, North Dakota. On exhibit were 150 Bronze, 30 White Holland, 26 Bourbon Red, and four Narragansett turkeys.

Breeders had to be cognizant of the intricate details of feather color, markings, and other elements of the purebred standards to sell to other breeders and fanciers, but they also needed to select stock with the economic traits desired by commercial producers. This division of purpose gradually led to the separation of most of the varieties into two populations, one for commercial production and one for exhibition purposes. As E. Y. Smith of Cornell University stated, "Even the coyotes don't eat the feathers." In spite of Smith's wry humor, early photographs reveal that the turkey probably looked better with its feathers on, as carcasses showed very prominent keel bones and slab-sided breasts. Its eating quality, however, was an original and continuing asset.

The development of the commercial industry

The Bronze variety, as the largest and most numerous of turkey varieties, attracted the most attention from breeders wanting to emphasize market characteristics, such as body size and breast width. The type of improved turkey which resulted was called the "Mammoth Bronze" to distinguish it from the Standard Bronze, which was selected for form and feather as described in the American Poultry Association's *Standard of Perfection.*

The rate of improvement of the Bronze variety began to accelerate early this century in the northwestern United States. By the 1920s, breeders in Washington and Oregon were producing larger birds with broader breasts. In 1926, an Englishman, Jesse Throssel, settled in British Columbia. The next

The Bronze received more attention than any other variety, whether breeders were selecting for show or utility qualities. Photo courtesy of Turkey World *magazine.*

year, he imported two lines of turkeys (a Bronze and a White) that had been selected for greater breast width. They were called the Cambridgeshire lines after the location of his home estate in England. By the late 1930s, Cambridgeshire Bronzes had been crossed with the Mammoth Bronzes in the northwestern United States. This mating proved auspicious, and it resulted in an even bigger, broader version of the Bronze variety. In 1938, a new organization was formed in the Northwest to concentrate on breeding for economic traits. Mrs. H. P. Griffin, wife of one of the

The Bourbon Red was still a viable commercial variety in the 1930s, when this photograph was taken, but it would soon be displaced by the new Broad-breasted Bronze. Photo courtesy of Turkey World *magazine.*

breeders in this club, coined the term "Broadbreasted Bronze" to describe the turkeys being bred.

Within a few years, North American turkeys were transformed by intensive selection within each population and through crossing with the improved Bronze stocks (Crawford 1984). "The heavy fleshing and blocky conformation produced an exceptionally attractive carcass which has met with great favor on the markets. The adoption of the Broadbreasted Bronze was phenomenal in its speed and completeness, practically replacing the Standard Bronze as a commercial variety within a period of five or six years following 1939. The fact that, from the standpoint of lean meat carried, the birds can be butchered profitably as early as ten weeks is a point stressed by the breeders. Due to larger size and distinctly different conformation, the large, broad-breasted turkeys [did] require some different measures of management, such as providing no roosts or very low roosts" (Marsden and Martin 1955). The new variety was quite similar in

color pattern to the Standard Bronze, but it had no specific requirements for markings. This was a major departure from the American Poultry Association's precise feather pattern requirements. The lack of uniformity present in the new variety made it an object of ridicule by many traditional Bronze breeders (Small 1974).

The period of the 1930s and 1940s was marked by heated arguments among breeders. Live bird "utility" classes and divisions for "dressed" turkeys (carcasses with feathers and blood removed) were added to the shows. Market characteristics were the only qualities considered in these classes. Eventually, dressed bird classes took over turkey exhibitions entirely, while classes for live turkeys were relegated to the multi-species poultry shows. Differences between advocates of "feather shows" versus dressed bird exhibitions became so intense that breeders of standard varieties threatened to cease advertising in *Turkey World* magazine unless it discontinued its energetic promotion of "utility" turkeys (Small 1974).

Bronze turkeys were raised on range in large numbers as recently as the 1960s. Photo courtesy of the Department of Animal and Veterinary Science, University of Maine.

Utility birds were soon the clear winners in this exchange, however, and the genetic potential they offered fueled dramatic market growth. The number of turkeys raised in the United States jumped from about 21 million in 1934 to 40 million in 1945. Production declined briefly following World War II, with 32 million turkeys produced in 1948, but it increased during the 1950s. In 1961, 127 million turkeys were produced (Small 1974).

Changes in turkey management accompanied economic expansion, though there were differences between regions. For example, in the Midwest, farmers kept birds indoors for the first twelve weeks and then put them on range. Range rearing was an important element in turkey production into the 1950s, as Marsden and Martin wrote in *Turkey Management* (1955), "Green grasses and legumes, when eaten by the birds from the range in liberal quantities, along with the sunshine simultaneously obtained, will satisfy the needs of turkeys (except for during the first few weeks of their lives) for all the essential vitamins and will make other important contributions in the form of minerals, carbohydrates, and proteins.

Because green feed and sunshine are cheaper than manufactured products, it is good management to make use of them whenever possible." The authors also cite a report from the Wisconsin Cooperative Extension Service which notes that "if turkeys are given good ladino range, they do not need antibiotics or B-12 after the age of six weeks." In other regions, however, range rearing was giving way to the use of outdoor pens built on porches to keep birds from contact with soil-borne organisms, or even indoor facilities. The ability to control disease was a necessity for keeping birds in close confinement.

Natural mating was still the norm, and it was expected that "when fertility is satisfactory, there will be no need to use artificial insemination" (Hamilton 1951). When Hamilton wrote his book, he encouraged farmers to choose varieties and develop their own breeding and selection programs to fit local and regional markets. Winter and Funk (1960) echoed this advice a decade later, suggesting that producers should select the turkey variety and breeding stock based on the needs of their markets, noting that there were many market traits other than size. They also commented on reproductive qualities, "Artificial insemination has become common practice among commercial breeders in order to ensure higher fertility of large sized, broader breasted varieties. This practice, though economically sound, is not recommended for replacement stock as there is a danger of developing strains that are unable to reproduce naturally."

The Broad-breasted Bronze variety was the dominant commercial bird of the time, though several other varieties were still seen, including the Standard Bronze, Bourbon Red, Narragansett, and White Holland. There was a problem, however, for the dark-feathered varieties. In the past, turkeys had been sold live and the buyer killed and processed them. Now, they were processed and packaged for the consumer, who made a choice based on the appearance of the carcass. Colored birds had dark pinfeathers, and melanin pigment was left in the feather follicles after plucking. White-feathered birds, such as the White Holland, had pin feathers which, though still present, were far less visible. The negative point for the white varieties was that they lacked the size of the Bronze.

Large, white-feathered birds became the goal. They were developed beginning in the 1950s from three origins: white "sports" occurring in the Bronze variety, line crosses of White Hollands with further selection for growth rate, and crosses of commercial lines of Bronze and White Holland (Small 1974). The resulting stocks became known as "Broad Whites" or "Large Whites." They began appearing on the market in the 1960s and soon eclipsed the Bronzes in popularity (Hawes 1998).

These changes in status can be illustrated by a comparison of advertisements in *Turkey World* magazine over several decades. A single issue of the magazine was chosen at random to represent the following years: 1930, 1941, 1971, and 1997. In the 1930 issue, there were a total of 166 ads. Of those, 68.2% were for Bronze turkeys, 9.4% for White Holland, 13.8% for Bourbon Red, and 8.6% for Narra-gansett, with no other varieties represented. In 1941, the percentage of ads was about the same for the Bronze variety (69.7%), while the White Holland doubled to 18.2%. This was an indication of preference for white feathers. Bourbon Red turkeys accounted for 6.1% and

White turkeys began to replace Bronze in the 1960s. Initially they were raised on range. Photo courtesy of Karl Nester.

The vast majority of Large White turkeys are now produced indoors. Photo courtesy of Turkey World *magazine.*

Blacks, 2%. In 1971, the Bronze variety accounted for 13% of the 27 ads, while the remainder (87%) featured a newcomer, the Large White. No other varieties were advertised. In 1997, only three ads appeared, all for the Large White and representing the three major turkey producing companies in the world.

The Large White is not a variety accepted by the American Poultry Association; in fact, none of the breeders ever made application for its recognition. There was no incentive for large breeding firms to create or maintain a recognized variety. Instead, it was the strains within the Large White population – each selected for certain production characteristics and marketed by company logo – that became the genetic units of importance as the industry grew. The turkey random sample tests of the 1950s began to offer side-by-side comparisons of the various strains available: Amerine, Browning, Gozzi, Jerome, Jones, Keithly, Kimber, Lovelace, Lyons, Nicholas, Rose-a-Linda and Wrolstad. The companies which developed these strains offered loosely arranged franchises to local hatcheries that would have otherwise bought eggs on the open market.

In 1966, there were approximately 116 million turkeys produced. Of these, 40 million were Broad-breasted Bronze, 60 million were Large White, and 15 million were Beltsville Small White. Other breeds made up the 1.5 million remainder (Marsden 1971). By 1970, confinement rearing had largely replaced the range rearing of turkeys, artificial insemination had become a standard practice, and the Large White dominated the turkey industry.

A change in the structure of the turkey industry was also occurring. The production of turkeys on diversified farms had declined in favor of specialized turkey farms with flocks of 1,000 to 10,000 birds. Nicholas Turkey Farm of Sonoma, California, founded in 1935, was among the first of these new businesses. Many small processing plants served this industry (Moreng 1995). Turkey production increased steadily during the 1950s. In 1961, however, a crash in prices pushed many of the smaller companies out of business. Another factor was whether or not companies were able to eliminate respiratory disease (*Mycoplasma gallisepticum*) from their flocks (Gascoyne 1989). The reduction in the number of businesses soon led to further concentration of interests. Vertical integration of all aspects of production, often initiated by large feed companies, took hold rapidly and has been the model of the turkey industry since then.

This shift from farmer-owned to company-owned breeding stock is apparent in a comparison of three books by Dr. Stanley Marsden. In the first edition of Marsden and Martin's book *Turkey Management* (1939), the goal was to help small producers achieve success given the new opportunities in this industry. The book provided information on every step in turkey production. The sixth edition, written in 1955, assumes that the producer starts with purchased day-old poults, though it still discusses the availability and usefulness of different varieties and has an extensive section on breeding and selection for those producers who want to manage their own breeding stocks or start a hatchery. In 1971, when Marsden wrote *Turkey Production*, there was no longer any comment on breeding or selection, because individual producers were simply no longer involved in this process.

The National Turkey Federation estimates that 270 million turkeys were produced in 1998. Growth of the industry has been based on an increasing year-around market for turkey (in school lunch programs, for example) and the importance of processed turkey as a deli meat and in sausage, hot dogs, and other products. Today, only about twenty percent of turkey sales are associated with the holiday season (Johnson 1998a). As a result, there are now two main products: "a small turkey, called a 'broiler' in North America, for home preparation and a heavy turkey for institutional use and further processing into convenience foods" (Crawford 1984).

The turkey industry is now concentrated economically, genetically, and geographically. The Large White variety accounts for well over 90% of the commercial market, and breeding stock is held primarily by three international companies: Nicholas Turkeys, British United Turkeys, and Hybrid Turkeys. These companies have their major farms in the United States, Canada, England, and Scotland, and they dominate turkey production in North America and Europe. They operate at all stages of turkey production, from selection of breeding

The consistency of Large White turkeys is an obvious production advantage but it also presents the challenges associated with genetic uniformity. Photo by Scott Bauer, courtesy of USDA-ARS.

stock to marketing the final products in the grocery store. Geographic concentration is reflected by the fact that, according to the USDA, over half of the turkeys produced in 1996 were raised in four states: North Carolina, Minnesota, Arkansas, and Virginia (Williams 1997).

The industry has had tremendous economic success based on total growth and volume of sales, but the overall profit margin is slender due to the low prices paid for turkey products. In 1997, for example, the wholesale price fell below the cost of production, and a drop in the export market caused significant market losses (Williams 1997).

The greatest problem facing the industry, however, may be the narrow genetic foundation of industrial turkeys. Intensive selection of a few strains of Large Whites has resulted in a highly efficient and consistent production of meat. At the same time, this strategy has also led to the increase in health problems such as ruptured aortas, joint and bone problems, and high blood pressure. Survival characteristics, such as disease resistance, have not been a pri-

ority. The uniformity of the turkey population presents its own problems. In the past, blights in corn, potatoes, and other crops have occurred because highly selected stocks were all vulnerable to the same diseases. It is possible that the industrial turkey population could be similarly vulnerable to a genetic disease or infectious organism.

The need to evaluate the status of turkey genetic diversity is attracting attention from poultry scientists (e.g. Ye 1998). Many are coming to realize that this diversity – in the form of rare varieties, university research flocks, and even some underutilized strains of Large White and Broad-breasted Bronze turkeys – must be conserved. These populations may be essential genetic resources if breeders are to be able to improve their birds' health and vigor or to respond to changing environmental conditions, production systems, or consumer needs. It is ironic but true that the most valuable turkeys of today are those which have something to offer for tomorrow.

Chapter 3

Turkey Genetic Diversity

"The need for conservation of genetic variability is perhaps more critical in the turkey than it is even for domestic chickens and is far more urgent than for most domesticated mammalian species."

—R. D. Crawford (1984)

THERE IS REASON TO BE CONCERNED about turkey genetic diversity. As described in the previous chapter, industrial turkeys in North America and Europe are produced from a relatively narrow background, that is, a few, highly selected strains of the Large White variety. These populations may lack the genetic diversity they need to be sustainable over the long term. In addition, industrial turkey strains are adapted to intensive husbandry and may not have the characteristics to thrive in other production systems (Beck-Chenowith 1996, Cramer 1993). Nor is it reasonable to expect them to. We cannot count on any single variety or breed to provide all of the genetic diversity a species will need for the future.

This leads to an obvious question: What other populations of turkeys should be conserved to protect genetic diversity? Historically, there have been a great many varieties of turkeys which have been useful genetic resources. Today, with the concentration of turkey production and the decline of small-scale turkey raising, all of these varieties are rare. Many are near extinction. The loss of these stocks would have a profound effect on the future health and utility of the turkey species.

The American Livestock Breeds Conservancy (ALBC), a national nonprofit organization, has taken the lead to research the status of non-industrial turkey varieties and encourage their conservation. ALBC was interested not only in the numeric and genetic status of the rare varieties, but also in access to these genetic resources. Are they available to farmers, fanciers, and breeders?

In addition to ALBC's census, the Society for the Preservation of Poultry Antiquities (SPPA), another conservation organization, has also completed a census of turkey varieties. Results are summarized later in this chapter.

Census of turkey varieties

During 1996 and 1997, the American Livestock Breeds Conservancy conducted a census in order to identify the rare turkey varieties that need to be conserved. This census followed the general methods of a previous census by ALBC (Christman and Heise 1987). Seasonal poultry hatcheries in the United States were surveyed to determine the status of the breeding populations of each variety. One of us (R. O. Hawes), then a poultry science professor at the University of Maine, initiated the project.

Traditional turkey varieties – now quite rare – must be conserved as genetic resources. This flock includes Taylor Bronze, Wolsted White, and Royal Palm. Photo by Don Bixby.

(See Hawes 1998.) Varieties were the focus of the study. The strains within each variety were also recognized as important, but they were not a part of this project.

Seasonal hatcheries (selling birds seasonally by mail) are in business to sell turkey varieties (and other poultry) to buyers across the United States. The hatchery business depends on the small-scale producer and the hobbyist. Yet each year, another business closes or a hatchery drops one or more of its turkey varieties. Everyone who is interested in turkeys has a vested interest in continued access to a diverse array of turkey varieties. No one should assume that "someone else" is saving the turkey stocks they may want in the future.

A census of poultry stocks is more difficult to perform than similar inventories of livestock. In the livestock species, one can gather information about breeds by contacting the various breed registries, since they keep annual records of population changes and ownership of animals (e.g. Bixby et. al. 1994). There are no such registries for poultry, however, so information must come from the hatcheries that sell each breed or variety. We contacted

each hatchery to ask the number of breeding males and females they were maintaining in each variety or for information about the source flocks they purchase stock from. After this was done, we estimated the total breeding population and number of breeding flocks of each variety that were being kept by the hatcheries as a group. The number of flocks was as important as the estimated total of birds because poultry are especially vulnerable to predation and disease; single flocks of almost any size can be lost overnight.

Poultry censuses may also be less accurate because of the relatively large number of birds in each flock and the relatively low economic value of each bird. Hatchery owners themselves may not know exactly how many birds they have at any given time, and population sizes can change quickly based on market demands or business directions. Nevertheless, a poultry census does give useful information on the relative popularity and prospects for each variety. It also establishes a baseline of comparison for results from similar studies in the future.

Twenty-five seasonal hatcheries in the

United States were the census population. Two of them were discontinuing turkeys, so the total number of hatcheries participating was actually twenty-three. These hatcheries represented almost all of the seasonal hatcheries selling turkey eggs and poults to the public. They provide stock for farmers, small scale producers, hobbyists, and exhibition breeders, but not for the larger-scale commercial producers or industrial farms, which keep their own stocks. The ALBC census did not include individuals raising turkeys.

The eight varieties recognized by the American Poultry Association were the subject of the census: Beltsville Small White, Black, Bourbon Red, Bronze, Narragansett, Royal Palm, Slate, and White Holland. A few other varieties, such as the Buff and Nebraskan, were asked about as well.

The census was conducted from 1995-1997. Ann Trundy and Jesse Babonis, students in the Department of Animal and Veterinary Sciences at the University of Maine, helped to gather information and made important contributions to the success of the project.

Results

Turkeys were not a major concern for most of the hatcheries. Though the majority of them sold one or more varieties, turkeys have certain characteristics, compared to chickens, that tend to make them less popular: they grow at a slower rate; they mature much later; they produce many fewer eggs (which lack a market as table eggs); and they require a greater amount of feed and space. Only one-third of the hatcheries surveyed – eight of twenty-three – actually raised their own turkey poults; the rest bought eggs from other hatcheries or private supply flocks. Two also bought poults for resale.

Of the eight hatcheries keeping their own turkey breeding flocks, five were raising the Bronze variety; one kept the Large White; and six maintained one or more of the rare varieties. The small number of hatcheries raising these varieties means that the genetic base is becoming fairly narrow. The five hatcheries carrying Bronze were not separated as to naturally-mating or artificially-mating stocks, though the Broad-breasted Bronze accounted for almost all of the total. One large hatchery

Seasonal hatcheries have an important role to play in making rare turkeys available to the public. Photo by Don Bixby.

supplied Bronze and Large White eggs for several of the smaller hatcheries.

The chart below shows the numbers of females by variety kept at the seasonal hatcheries. These are the breeding birds which would normally be kept for the next season. In most cases, the number of males would be about 10% of the female number. The Broad-breasted type of the Bronze variety was the most popular with the small flock owner, and it was sold by most of the hatcheries, but only five of them are maintaining their own breeding stock. Although the number of breeding females (7,038) appeared encour-

aging, one hatchery owned about 90% of that total, leaving only 10% (about 640) divided among the other four.

Of the remaining varieties, the Bourbon Red was the most numerous, with five hatcheries owning 664 females. The Royal Palm was found at four hatcheries with a total of 381 females. Black turkeys were being raised at three hatcheries with a total of 62 females, and the Slates at two hatcheries with 60 females. The Narragansett was being kept at only one hatchery which has three females (as well as a few males), making this wonderful historic variety practically extinct at the seasonal

Rare Turkey Varieties at Seasonal Hatcheries

This chart summarizes the ALBC Census results. A total of 23 hatcheries were selling turkeys in 1997. The first column shows how many hatcheries were selling each variety. The second column shows how many hatcheries were maintaining their own breeding stock. The third column estimates the total number of females.

Variety	Hatcheries Selling Turkeys (23)	Hatcheries Maintaining Breeders (8)	# of Females
Bronze *	22	5	7,038*
Large White	5	1	4,600
Bourbon Red	10	5	664
Royal Palm	8	4	381
Black	4	3	62
Slate	2	2	60
Narragansett	1	1	3
White Holland	1	1	4

* includes both Broad-breasted and Standard Bronze

Seasonal Hatcheries Surveyed

Abendroth Waterfowl Hatchery, Waterloo, WI; Cackle Hatchery, Lebanon, MO; Clearview Hatchery, Gratz, PA; Dunlap Hatchery, Caldwell, ID; Eagle Nest Hatchery, Oeola, OH; Grain Belt Hatchery, Windsor, MO; Harder's Hatchery, Ritzville, WA; Hoffman Hatchery, Gratz, PA; Hoover's Hatchery, Rudd, IA; Ideal Poultry Breeding Farm, Cameron, TX; Inman Hatchery, Aberdeen, SD; Kent Turkey Hatchery, Johnson City, TX; Kruse Hatchery, Fort Atkinson, IA; Marti's Hatchery, Windsor, MO; Mother Goose Hatchery, Middlebury, IN; Mount Healthy Hatchery, Mt Healthy, OH; Murray McMurray Hatchery, Webster City, IA; Privette's Hatchery, Portales, NM; Protection Hatchery, Pratt, KS; Ridgeway Hatchery, LaRue, OH; Sand Hill Preservation Center, Calamus, IA; Shank's Hatchery, Hubbard, OR; Stork Hatchery and Farm Store, Fredericksburg, IA; Sun Ray Chicks, Hazelton, IA; Wish Poultry, Prairie City, OR. For sources for turkey varieties, including addresses, see the Hatchery list at the end of the book.

hatcheries. Fortunately, Narragansetts are also being raised by individual breeders. Both the White Hollands and the Beltsville Small Whites were found at only one hatchery.

This census focused only on the eight recognized varieties, but many others have been documented in the past, including the Auburn, Black-wing Bronze, Buff, Nebraskan, Nittany, Grey, and Silver Auburn. Of these, only the Beltsville Small White, Buff, and Nebraskan were queried about. None of these was found initially at the hatcheries, but some of the varieties were later located at one hatchery, Sand Hill Preservation Center. We do know that many of these are also being maintained by individuals, though in most cases the popu-lations are even smaller than those of the recognized varieties.

Conclusions and conservation needs

Seasonal hatcheries have a vitally important part to play in turkey conservation. As a group, the hatcheries in the United States offer eight or more varieties of turkeys for the small-scale producer or fancier. None of the hatcheries we surveyed are purposefully doing any cross-breeding, meaning that the varieties are being kept in a pure state. Strictly speaking, genetic diversity is being maintained, but most of the varieties are critically rare, and they are found at only a small number of the hatcheries.

While these results address the questions

SPPA Turkey Census

In 1998, the Society for the Preservation of Poultry Antiquities (SPPA) conducted its own census of turkey varieties through an inventory of hatchery and individual flock owners. This census was a good complement to ALBC research because it updated hatchery information and also included responses from many individual flock owners. The results were quite consistent with ALBC figures. Though larger numbers were found for some varieties, there was still the problem of a limited number of flocks in every variety. For example, half of the Narragansetts are owned by two hatcheries, and almost half of the Slates are owned by one hatchery. The results on the recognized varieties are listed below. The SPPA also located small numbers of birds in other varieties, including Auburn, Chocolate, Lilac, and Silver Auburn. This is encouraging, though more breed-ers are needed for all of the varieties if they are to survive.

Black	164 females	(62 in ALBC census)
Bourbon Red	782 females	(664 in ALBC census)
Standard Bronze	281 females	(not available in ALBC census)
Narragansett	70 females	(3 in ALBC census)
Royal Palm	589 females	(381 in ALBC census)
Slate	108 females	(60 in ALBC census)
White Holland	22 females	(4 in ALBC census)

Paula Johnson, author of the census, and her colleagues at the SPPA are to be com-mended for their efforts to document the status of rare varieties and make a strong case for their conservation. A copy of the report is available from the SPPA; see the address in the Sources of Information list.

Living populations of turkeys are our only gene banks for the future, so it is important to ask who is producing the next generation. These are Wishard Bronze poults. Photo by David Sullenberger.

of numerical status, there are also issues of genetic status to be considered. For example, how closely related are the hatchery strains of each variety? Are the hatcheries conducting a selection program to keep pressure on the marketable traits? Is it enough to merely preserve a variety based on feather color alone? If there is little or no concern for conformation, egg production, or growth rate, how well are the interests of that variety being served? Appropriate selection must be a part of any long term conservation effort, and it is not known to what extent this is occurring. The Beltsville Small White, Buff, Slate, and White Holland populations pose some specific genetic questions. Are these populations distinct and consistent enough to be considered true varieties in the genetic sense? They merit further study.

Individual breeders play an essential role in turkey conservation. Buying poults each year supports conservation by strengthening the market for rare varieties. Raising flocks year-round, selecting for appropriate type and performance characteristics, and hatching out replacements is direct conservation. Documentation of what rare varieties can do is also needed, as this type of information would be of great help in promoting these turkeys to new audiences. Making birds available to other breeders and starting new conservation flocks are the last pieces of the puzzle. In all of these ways, individual breeders are working to conserve rare varieties.

Chapter 4

Rare Turkey Varieties

"I can't speak for the nation, but here in Pennsylvania before World War II, most general purpose farms had a few turkeys. Mostly these were Standard Bronze, but a good many Narragansett could also be found. Some individuals kept Blacks, Slates, Reds, Buffs, Whites, or even some of the rare, non-standard colors or hybrid flocks ... Poultry was the most diverse segment of livestock operations."

—Craig Russell (1991)

IN MOST SPECIES OF POULTRY and livestock, the term "breed" describes a group of animals that are distinctive in conformation, color, performance, behavior, and other qualities. Each breed has a unique combination of these characteristics. Its consistency of appearance reflects an underlying genetic consistency, so that when individuals of the same breed are mated together, they reproduce the same distinct type. That is, breeds breed true.

Some breeds of chickens, ducks, and geese have sub-breed populations which show variations in color (and in the case of chickens, comb type and feather type as well). These are called "varieties." They are similar in form and function to other varieties in the breed.

The turkey species is classified differently. The American Poultry Association (APA) considers the domestic turkey to be a single breed with eight varieties: Black, Bronze, Narragansett, Slate, White Holland, Bourbon Red, Beltsville Small White, and Royal Palm. The first five of these were recognized by APA in its original *Standard of Perfection* in 1874. The remaining three were accepted later based on a system whereby breeders applied for recognition and then held a "qualifying meet" at a designated show. In addition to these eight varieties, there are several others which are not recognized by the APA, presumably due to their being kept in small numbers and the breeders not having applied for recognition. One variety, the Buff, was originally recognized by the APA but has been dropped. This variety is now enjoying a revival of interest and should perhaps be considered for readmittance.

A disadvantage of this terminology is that "variety" does not have a consistent genetic meaning. Some turkey varieties are distinctive and should be considered genetic populations similar to the breeds in the other species. These include the Standard Bronze, Bourbon Red, Black, and Narragansett. Others, such as the Auburn and Silver Auburn, are merely colorful variations on the same theme, with one or more feather pattern or feather color mutations their only hallmark. They are more like the varieties of the other species. Others fall somewhere in between, and more study is needed to find out where they fit.

ALBC Conservation Priority Turkey Varieties

Critical Fewer than 1,000 breeding females in the United States, with five or fewer primary breeding flocks (100 females)

Rare Fewer than 2,000 breeding females in the United States, with seven or fewer primary breeding flocks

Watch Fewer than 10,000 breeding females in the United States, with ten or fewer primary breeding flocks

Study Varieties which are of genetic interest but need more documentation

Critical	Rare	Watch	Study
Black		Broad-breasted	Beltsville Small White
Bourbon Red		Bronze	Buff
Standard Bronze			Slate
Narragansett			White Holland
Royal Palm			

In this chapter, you will see some varieties described as "well documented." These varieties have a persistent breed identity described, from the time of their origins, in a range of books, periodicals, hatchery catalogs, fair and show results, and other historic records. In addition, the living populations have the same characteristics that were documented in the past. Most of the varieties which are not well documented are likely to be color phases of other varieties. These can be interesting and worthwhile if they show unique color patterns or especially if there is a chance that they are remnants of historic populations.

The character of the varieties is important in determining appropriate conservation strategies for them. Established, genetically consistent populations should be managed as pure breeds. Color varieties can be managed with less attention to pure breeding while maintaining their distinctive hues and patterns. In the future, biological technologies (such as blood typing and DNA techniques used in other species) may provide a more precise way to document the genetic status and relationships of rare turkey varieties. One recent study in this regard was done at Ohio State University (Ye et. al. 1998). It compared the genetic relationship between some elite industrial strains of Large Whites and the research strains of Large White being maintained at OSU. Until such work extends to some of the standard varieties, historical research and phenotypic comparisons of various populations are our only options for evaluating rare and historic strains.

This chapter includes descriptions of the history, characteristics, and status of each recognized variety (The Buff is also included, even though it is not currently a recognized variety.) There is also a short discussion of other varieties and colors. Data from ALBC's census and the SPPA census were combined to give the most up-to-date information possible. Hatchery sources for each variety are listed in the back of the book.

Beltsville Small White

The Beltsville Small White was developed by the U.S. Department of Agriculture research center in Beltsville, Maryland, between 1934 and 1941. The goal was to produce a small, white-feathered turkey, early maturing and easily reproduced, for home and small-scale production. The variety was selected from a genetic foundation which included the White Holland, White Austrian, Narragansett, Bronze, and Wild turkey.

The Beltsville variety came into wide use in the 1940s, and it was recognized by the American Poultry Association in 1951. The height of its popularity came in the mid-1950s, when an estimated nineteen million Beltsville Small White turkeys were raised in the United States (Marsden 1967). In addition to its use as a purebred, the Beltsville Small White also contributed to the development of other strains of medium and small white turkeys, though these populations were never very well defined.

The Beltsville Small White had only short-lived success, however, and within twenty years of its greatest popularity, it was practically extinct (Small 1974). Although considered a fine bird for family use, it was less well received by the hotel and restaurant trade. The Beltsville was replaced by the Large White, which, when slaughtered at a young age, was of the right size to fit the processor's niche for a smaller turkey but could also be grown to target weights for the commercial food trade. There was, of course, an obvious disadvantage for the farmer in this exchange. The Beltsville Small White had good reproductive qualities (including natural mating ability) and so could be selected, bred, and maintained by small-scale producers. In contrast, Large White turkeys generally require artificial insemination for reproduction.

According to the APA *Standard*, mature Beltsville Small White toms weigh 21–23 pounds and old hens 12–13 pounds. ("Mature" means one year or older and it corresponds with the term "old" used by the American Poultry Association in the *Standard of Perfection*.) The plumage is pure white. The beard is black, and the beak is horn colored. The eyes are brown, and the shanks and toes are pinkish-white.

In recent years, there has been a revival of interest in this variety. Efforts are underway to locate and conserve any remnant flocks in the United States and Canada. In addition, a population of approximately 100 White Midgets turkeys (which may be related to the historic Beltsville type) has been located at the University of Wisconsin (Johnson 1998b).

Status: Study. More information about this variety is needed.

Beltsville Small White turkeys were selected as a compact, white-feathered variety for small-scale production. Note the size in contrast to the Standard Bronze. This photograph was taken in 1941 and is used courtesy of Turkey World *magazine.*

The Black variety was a foundation for the Bronze, Narragansett, and Slate varieties. Photo by Phillip Sponenberg.

Black

The Black variety originated in Europe from Mexican turkeys which had been imported beginning in the 1500s. Black-colored turkeys became especially popular in Spain and later in the Norfolk region of England. Though little is known about the *Negra de Pavos* (black turkeys of Spain), a well-documented and distinct black variety was developed in England. It was called the Norfolk Black, for its home region, and celebrated for the quality of its meat.

Black turkeys were originally described as being dull in color with no sheen. Many of them were not even solid black but had white tips on their tail feathers. The skin had a yellow tinge that distinguished it from other varieties. Dressed black turkeys were described by Cline (1929) as having "… a very pleasing appearance because they are usually smaller and plumper than the larger breeds, having more the appearance of a fat chicken hen."

After two centuries in England, Norfolk Black turkeys returned to the Americas with European colonists. These turkeys, when crossed with wild birds, were a foundation for

the Bronze, Narragansett, and Slate varieties, as well as being the basis for the Black variety in America. The Black was recognized by the American Poultry Association in 1874, and it was popular and well known. Breeders selected for a calm disposition, early maturation, and rapid growth rate. Further development also included periodic matings back to a Bronze line. The resulting Black offspring added both hybrid vigor and increased size to the Black populations. The Black variety remained commercially popular until the middle of this century, when the Broad-breasted Bronze became dominant.

Black turkeys are lustrous, metallic black with a greenish sheen. It is undesirable to have a brownish or bronze cast or any white edging on the feathers. Poults often have white or bronze in their feathers but molt into mature plumage. The beak is slaty black, and the eyes are dark brown. Shanks and toes are usually black, although the APA *Standard* calls for pink shanks and toes. Standard weights are 33 pounds for mature toms and 18 pounds for mature hens. In contrast to the standard for American turkeys, Black turkeys in Britain retain the traditional dull black feathering and always have black shanks and toes.

The terms "Norfolk Black" and "Black Spanish" are sometimes seen today, though they are confusing. Perhaps an assumption is being made that leg color distinguishes the two types, with pink associated with a Spanish strain and black with the Norfolk strain. It seems unlikely, however, that two distinct strains of Black turkeys have been maintained over such a long time. It is more reasonable to consider all Black turkeys to be included in a single Black variety today.

The Black turkey is critically rare. Its potential for small-scale production today is unexplored, though it merits evaluation for use in such niches. Expanded use in agriculture, as well as breeding by fanciers, would enhance this historic variety's chances for survival.

Status: Critical. There are approximately 100–160 hens of this variety in the United States.

Bourbon Red

The Bourbon Red turkey is named for Bourbon County in Kentucky's Bluegrass region, where it originated in the late 1800s. It was developed by J. F. Barbee from crosses between Buff, Bronze, and White Holland turkeys. The initial steps actually took place in Pennsylvania, where Buff turkeys of darker red hues – called Tuscarora or Tuscawara – were bred and then taken west with settlers bound for Ohio and Kentucky (Russell 1991, 1998). These dark Buff turkeys would be the primary foundation for the new variety.

After some years of selection, Mr. Barbee was able to produce consistently good-sized, dark red turkeys with white wing and main tail feathers. He christened them "Bourbon Butternuts." For some reason, perhaps because the name did not appeal to the public, the birds did not attract attention. Barbee then rechristened them "Bourbon Reds," Bourbon for his home county and red for the rich, chestnut color of the plumage. The name change seemed to work, and better sales were reported.

The Bourbon Red was named for Bourbon County, Kentucky, where it was developed early this century. Photo by Phillip Sponenberg.

The Bourbon Red variety was recognized by the American Poultry Association in 1909. It was ambitiously selected and promoted for utility traits, including a production-type conformation with a heavy breast and richly-flavored meat. Early breeders of the Bourbon Red also claimed that their birds would grow as large as any Mammoth Bronze. L. E. Cline, author of *Turkey Production* (1929), wrote that the Bourbon Red is "one of the most recent turkey breeds ... now rapidly growing in favor." Ironically, the rise of the Bourbon Red accompanied the decline of the Buff, which had been removed from the APA's *Standard of Perfection* in 1915.

Like others of the time, Bourbon Red breeders faced a challenge in balancing the utility and exhibition points of their birds. This topic is discussed in the November 1932 issue of *Turkey World*. Clara Fero, a Bourbon Red breeder of Whitewater, Wisconsin, wrote, "The Fair season is over and we are now looking forward to the big winter shows. By showing our birds at the Fair, where the commercial side plays a mighty factor, and at the large shows where the show qualities are considered, we are assured our stock measures up to both standards." Breeders were successful, and the Bourbon Red was an important commercial variety through the 1930s and 1940s. After this time, however, it declined in commercial importance as it was unable to compete with the broad-breasted varieties.

Bourbon Red turkeys have dark red plumage with white in the flight and tail feathers. The main tail feathers are crossed by a soft red bar near the end. Body feathers on the toms may be edged in black, though the less black, the better. The neck and breast feathers are chestnut mahogany, with a narrow edging of white present on the breast feathers of the females. The under feathers are light red shading to light salmon. The beak is light horn at the tip and dark at base, and the eyes are dark brown. The beard is black, and the shanks and toes are reddish pink. Standard weights are 33 pounds for mature toms and 18 pounds for mature hens.

Bourbon Reds are active foragers and should do well in pasture-based turkey production systems. The light pinfeathers mean a clean carcass, another advantage. Conservationists could make a contribution by documenting this variety's performance ability and promoting it into appropriate niches in sustainable agriculture.

Status: Critical. There are approximately 600–700 breeding hens of the Bourbon Red variety in the United States.

Bronze – Standard and Broad-breasted

The Bronze has been the most popular turkey variety for most of American history. It originated from crosses between the domestic turkeys brought by European colonists to the Americas and the Eastern wild turkeys they found upon their arrival. The hybrid vigor of this cross resulted in turkey stocks that were larger and more vigorous than the European birds, and they were also much tamer than wild turkeys. The metallic sheen which gives the variety its name was part of the inheritance from its wild ancestors.

Bronze turkeys have an iridescent green bronze on the surface of the blackish feathers covering the neck, breast, wing bows, secondary coverts, and back. Feathers in most of this area end in a black band, and body feathers end with a narrow white edging. The primary and secondary flight feathers are marked with alternate black and white bars. The tail feathers are dull black, each marked with parallel lines of brown and having a wide black band near the end which terminates in a white edging. Females have additional white edging to the feathers over the back, wing bows, wing coverts, breast, and body. The beard is black, and the shanks and toes are smoky pink. According to weights in the APA *Standard*, mature toms weigh up to 36 pounds and mature hens up to 20 pounds.

Bronze-type turkeys were known by the late 1700s, but the name "Bronze" did not formally appear until the 1830s when it was used to describe the Point Judith Bronze turkey, a local strain developed in the vicinity of Point Judith, Rhode Island (Robinson 1924). Throughout the 1800s, breeders began to standardize the Bronze, and occasional crosses were made back to the wild turkey. The Bronze variety was recognized by the American Poultry Society in 1874.

By 1900, the systematic selection of Bronze turkeys for greater breast width and larger size had created a "Mammoth Bronze" type which was beginning to diverge from the "Standard Bronze," selected according to the APA *Standard* as well as for production traits. In the early 1900s, breeders in the northwestern United States took the lead in further improvement of the Bronze, including crossing with broader-breasted English Bronze turkeys which had been imported to Canada in 1927. This led to the development of the Broad-breasted type of Bronze in America, which was distinguished by "extremely heavy muscular

The Bronze has historically been the most popular variety in America. This is a Wishard strain male. Photo by David Sullenberger.

37

Standard Bronze strains have been selected according to the 1874 APA Standard. This is a Kardosh strain male. Photo by Frank Reese.

development, especially on breast and legs" and greater feed efficiency, though laying ability and hatchability tended to be lower" (Marsden and Martin 1955). Broad-breasted Bronze tended to be darker with less distinct markings than Standard Bronze, but they could not be accurately distinguished by feather color alone.

By the 1940s, the Broad-breasted Bronze had replaced the Standard Bronze to become the dominant commercial turkey across North America. One result of the changes in conformation (especially the shorter legs and the broader breast) was the near elimination of the turkeys' ability to mate naturally, requiring that the vast majority of Broad-breasted Bronze turkeys be artificially inseminated.

Twenty years later, in the 1960s, the Broad-breasted Bronze was itself replaced by the newly developed Large White turkey. Processors favored the white-feathered variety because of its light pinfeathers and visually cleaner carcass, and the Large White now accounts for the vast majority of turkeys produced. The Broad-breasted Bronze is used only sparingly as a commercial strain, though some of the breeding companies maintain small

numbers of Bronze as a genetic resource. It does remain popular for seasonal small-scale and home production. (A hatchery manager speculated that this was because people enjoy the appearance of the darker birds more than the white ones, which tend to get dirty and stay that way. It also implies that people aren't dissuaded from raising their own Bronze turkeys by the color of the pinfeathers.)

The naturally-mating Standard Bronze has been left even farther behind by the turkey industry, and it is critically rare. All Standard Bronze strains, such as the historic Kardosh line, urgently need conservation. There are also a few rare strains of range-selected, naturally mating Bronze. Though not technically considered Standard Bronze because they have not been actively selected according to the 1874 Standard, these strains are similar enough to be loosely grouped together. The best-known is the Wishard strain from Wish Poultry of Prairie City, Oregon, which was begun in 1946. Today, Wish Poultry maintains about 120 females and 30 males.

Another obstacle in the conservation of the Standard Bronze is the standard for the variety. In 1940, a nod was given to the commecial stocks, and the APA *Standard* now states that the birds are "sometimes referred to in modern commercial technology as Broad-breasted Bronze." Standard weights are larger than the historic Standard types but smaller than the industrial types. It is interesting to note that the British poultry standards distinguish between the Broad-breasted Bronze and the Standard Bronze, no longer considering them as one variety. A similar change in the United States might encourage the breeding of Standard Bronze turkeys and thus support their conservation.

Status of Standard Bronze: Critical. The Society for the Preservation of Poultry Antiquities reports fewer than 300 Standard Bronze females.

Status of Broad-breasted Bronze: Watch. Though this type is far more numerous, with an estimated 7,000 females at the seasonal hatcheries, its population is held in a very limited number of flocks. Hatcheries serving the turkey industry were not surveyed, so it is not known how many Bronze are found there. These, however, are generally not available to the public.

Buff

The Buff is named for the rich reddish-buff color of its body feathers. Tail feathers are white with a light buff bar across them near the end. Primary and secondary wing feathers are white with buff shading. The shanks and toes are bluish-white or flesh colored, and the beard is black. The eyes are hazel. Mature toms weigh about 25 pounds and mature hens about 15 pounds. This variety presents a beautiful picture, but it was also selected for good reproductive and market qualities. Its creamy white under-feathers were an advantage in processing. The Buff was recognized by the American Poultry Association in 1874 and historically had its strongest population in the mid-Atlantic states.

Buff turkeys from Pennsylvania were used in the development of the Bourbon Red variety early in this century. The Bourbon Red, selected more purposefully for performance and promoted more widely, gained prominence, and the Buff declined. By the early 1900s, it had become rare. One obstacle for the variety was the difficulty of breeding birds

The Buff turkey is one of the rarest varieties today. Photo by Phillip Sponenberg.

to fit the Buff color standard. In 1915, the Buff turkey was removed from the American Poultry Association's *Standard of Perfection*.

Interest in the Buff turkey was revived during the 1940s and 1950s, when the New Jersey Agricultural Experiment Station at Millville used Buffs in its project to improve small to medium size turkeys. Emphasis was placed on the development of turkeys with good reproductive and market qualities. This was successful, and for some time, Buffs – then called Jersey Buffs – became popular again. For example, in 1951, the Jersey Buff was the fourth most popular variety raised in the United States. (This was about the same time that the Beltsville Small White variety was also attracting attention.) The use of small and medium sized varieties declined, however, in favor of the use of Large Whites, which, if slaughtered at a young age could meet processors' requirements.

Today the Buff variety is close to extinction, and it is available at only one hatchery in the United States. Efforts are underway to locate additional remnant flocks and increase the number of breeders. At the same time, this variety also merits more study to see if there is a documented relationship between Buff turkeys of today and historical populations.

Status: Study, as more information is needed. The Buff has an estimated population of fewer than 100 hens.

Narragansett

The Narragansett turkey is named for Narragansett Bay in Rhode Island, where it was developed. It descends from a cross between wild turkeys and domestic birds (probably Norfolk Blacks) brought to the American colonies by English and European colonists beginning in the 1600s. Improved and standardized for production qualities, this variety became the foundation of the historic turkey industry in New England. It was especially important in Rhode Island and Connecticut, though it was valued across the region and later around the country. The Narragansett was recognized by the American Poultry Association in 1874.

An early account of the Narragansett variety in New England by an anonymous writer was published in *The Poultry World* of December 1872. According to the account, it was apparently not uncommon to find flocks of one to two hundred birds, the product of a breeder flock of about a dozen hens. There was little feed given to the turkeys; instead, they ranged for grasshoppers, crickets, and other insects. Farmers raising the turkeys were aware of the positive consequences of genetic

The Narragansett is the oldest turkey variety developed in the United States, but it is now close to extinction. Photo by Frank Reese, Jr.

selection and were raising young gobblers that would weigh 22–28 pounds and hens that would weigh 12–16 pounds.

The Narragansett was never as popular as the Bronze variety, but it was widely known in the Midwest and mid-Atlantic as well as in New England. Since the early1900s, however, the Narragansett has declined relative to the Bronze, especially the Broad-breasted Bronze. It has not been a commercial variety for many decades. The Narragansett population is very small today, and its potential use for small-scale turkey production is unexplored.

The Narragansett color pattern is made up of black, gray, tan, and white. Its pattern is similar to that of the Bronze, with steel gray or dull black replacing the copper bronze. Wing bars are white. This pattern results from a genetic mutation which removes the bronzing coloration; it is not known outside the United States. Breeders may be interested to know that as day-old poults, Narragansetts are indistinguishable from Bronze. The beak of the Narragansett is horn colored, the beard is black, and the shanks and feet are salmon pink. Standard weights are 33 pounds for mature toms and 20 pounds for mature hens.

Narragansett turkeys have traditionally been known for their calm disposition, good maternal abilities, early maturation, and excellent egg production. As recently as 50 years ago, they were well regarded for production qualities, though in recent decades have neared extinction. This historic variety, unique to North America, merits evaluation for production in sustainable agriculture and use as an exhibition and farm bird. It deserves to survive.

Status: Critical. There are fewer than 100 Narragansett turkeys alive today.

Royal Palm

The Royal Palm is a strikingly attractive and small-sized turkey variety. The first birds in American to have the Palm color pattern appeared in a mixed flock of Black, Bronze, Narragansett, and Wild turkeys on the farm of Enoch Carson of Lake Worth, Florida, in the 1920s. Further selection has been made since then to stabilize the consistency of color and other characteristics. As an anonymous breeder wrote to *Feathered World* magazine in 1931, "Turkeys of this type of coloration do crop up by chance where different color varieties are crossed … but it takes years to perfect their markings." The Royal Palm was recognized by the American Poultry Association in 1971. The Royal Palm is similar to a European variety called the Pied, Crollwitz, or Black-laced White, which has been known since the 1700s.

Royal Palm turkeys are white with a sharply contrasting, metallic black edging on the feathers. The saddle is black and the tail is

Royal Palm turkeys are small, active, and thrifty. Photo by Phillip Sponenberg.

The Slate turkey, also known as the Blue Slate or Lavender, presents the challenge of getting the color just right. Photo by Phillip Sponenberg.

pure white, with each feather having a band of black and an edge of white. The coverts are white with a band of black, and the wings are white with a narrow edge of black on each feather. The breast is white with the exposed portion of each feather ending in a band of black to form a contrast of black and white similar to the scales of a fish. The turkeys have deep pink shanks and toes, light brown eyes, and black beards.

Royal Palms are active, thrifty turkeys, excellent foragers and good flyers. Standard weights are 22 pounds for mature toms and 12 pounds for mature hens. The Royal Palm has not been purposefully selected for either growth rate or muscling, being used primarily as an ornamental variety. As a result, it has been used commercially on only a limited basis. It may, however, have a role to play on small farms, for home production of meat or where pest control is one of the priorities.

Status: Critical, with an estimated population of 380 breeding hens held by the seasonal hatcheries in the United States. There may be 300 more hens owned by individual breeders.

Slate

The Slate or Blue Slate variety is named for its color, solid to ashy blue over the entire body, with or without a few black flecks. It has also been called the Blue or Lavender turkey. Hens are lighter in hue than the toms. The beak is horn in color, the eyes are dark brown, and the beard is black. The shanks and toes are pink. Standard weights are 33 pounds for mature toms and 18 pounds for mature hens.

The Slate was accepted by the American Poultry Association in 1874. It resembles the Black turkey and may well have been derived from that variety or from a cross between the Black and the White Holland. One added element of confusion in defining the variety is that there are actually two different genetic mutations (one dominant and one recessive) that produce the blue slate color, and these produce slightly different shades. White and rusty brown markings may be present but are considered a defect.

The Slate has not been used commercially to any extent, but it has been popular in exhibition circles. This variety is, however, less well documented, more variable in type and color, and more challenging to breed consistently than the others. Its production potential today is not known.

Status: Study, as more information about the variety's genetic status is needed. The Slate is critically rare, with an estimated population of 60–100 breeding hens in the United States.

White Holland

The White Holland was the most important white-feathered variety throughout most of American history. Despite this illustrious past, the White Holland is one of the rarest and most difficult to authenticate varieties today.

The mutation to the white color (which is actually a lack of color) is an ancient one. The Aztecs and others selectively bred white turkeys, and they were certainly among the stocks sent to Europe. In Austria and in Holland, white turkeys were favored. It is quite possible, though not documented, that Dutch settlers or other European immigrants came to the New World with white turkeys. By the 1800s, a white variety – now called the White Holland in the show ring – was known in the United States. It was recognized by the American Poultry Association in 1874.

The name White Holland implied Dutch origins for the variety, but regardless of the nature of the original population, it was no doubt changed significantly once in the United States, through selection for production qualities and with

the introduction of white "sports" from Bronze flocks. Writers of the era debated the distinctiveness of the White Holland, but the continued development of its vitality and size was seen as evidence of hybrid vigor from the cross. The White Holland became a popular variety, especially in New England, and held its own well into this century. Though less numerous than the Bronze and smaller in size, the White Holland demonstrated earlier maturation and offered a cleaner carcass than dark-colored birds.

However, producers came to want the best of both worlds – a large, white feathered variety. In the early 1950s, researchers at Cornell University and elsewhere in the United States began to develop one by crossing the White Holland and Broad-breasted Bronze. By the 1960s, the "Broad-breasted White" (or "Large White") had surpassed the Bronze for commercial production, and it dominates the turkey industry today.

The White Holland, as a distinctive and historic population, is close to extinction. White Holland turkeys are seen occasionally

White Holland. Drawing by F. L. Sewell.

at poultry shows, but they often have the wide breasts and short legs reflecting genetic influence from the Large White. The American Poultry Association both recognized this fact and confused the issue in 1983, when a change in the White Holland standard added the following: "May be referred to in commercial terminolgy as Broad-breasted Whites or Large Whites." Thus, the two varieties have been merged, with the White Holland absorbed into the Large White. The same thing has occurred in Britain, with the lumping of all white varieties into a population called the "British White" turkey.

Breeders of today are debating the status of the White Holland variety: Does it survive? If so, how can the remnants be conserved? A good place to start would be the documentation of the birds curently known as White Hollands. Do they have the consistency of appearance and performance expected of a pure variety? Do they have characteristics that are distinct from Large Whites? Perhaps DNA technologies will be of value in answering these questions in the future.

The White Holland turkey should have snow white feathers, free from cream and other off-colors. The beard is black; the beak is pink to horn colored; the throat and wattles are pinkish-white; and the eyes are dark brown or occasionally blue. Shanks and toes are pinkish white. Standard weights are 36 pounds for mature toms and 20 pounds for mature hens.

Status: Study, as more information about this variety is needed. This variety is likely to be critically rare. The SPPA census estimated 50–100 females alive today.

Case Study: Sweetgrass Turkeys

Genetic conservation can be full of surprises. It's often the case that we have to act quickly to save a population before we can be sure about its long term importance. Such rescue opportunities are usually expensive, both in money and in time, and they require a network of participants to share the benefits and responsibilities. Conservation of the Sweetgrass turkeys is a good case study of such a project.

In 1993, Sweetgrass Farms in Big Timber, Montana, began a commercial flock of free range turkeys. The foundation stock was made up primarily of Wishard strain Bronze from Wish Poultry in Prairie City, Oregon, with some birds from a Bronze research flock at Oregon State University. The choice of varieties was a good one, and the turkeys proved to be hardy and productive in this rugged environment. There was strong consumer demand for the high-quality meat. The only obstacle was the lack of a federally inspected processing facility. The birds had to be transported to California for processing.

A new development in the story occurred in 1996, when some light colored poults were produced by the conventionally colored Bronze parents. These poults were placed into a separate flock and, when bred together, they reproduced the same light color – a heavily marked Royal Palm pattern with chestnut red in the toms' tails. In 1997 and 1998, more of the light poults were produced. They seemed to be every bit as hardy as their Bronze colored cousins. The birds had significant value, because the underfeathers were white, producing as clean a carcass as if the birds had been solid white.

Despite its ability to produce good turkeys, Sweetgrass Farms decided to discontinue its turkey enterprise in 1998. The problem was the processing bottleneck: the owner decided that the only way to make

The Sweetgrass turkey strain may find its niche in sustainable agriculture. Photo courtesy of Ray Suiter.

the project commercially viable was to build his own federally inspected processing facility, and this wasn't something he was prepared to do. He called ALBC for advice on selling the turkeys, especially the light colored ones.

ALBC decided to try to save the Sweetgrass Farms strain if at all possible. As range-selected, naturally-mating turkeys they were quite unusual; as Wishard Bronze descendants, they were a conservation priority; and, their unusual color meant that the turkeys might fit a sustainable agriculture niche. With the financial support of the Kind World Foundation, ALBC was able to purchase a portion of the flock to establish two conservation flocks.

Beside the immediate rescue, there were two other goals: find breeders who could evaluate the strain and could also make birds available to others in the future. Glenn Drowns of Sand Hill Preservation Center in Calamus, Iowa, and Andy Lee of Good Earth Farm in Buena Vista, Virginia, agreed to take flocks. Phillip Sponenberg of ALBC visited Sweetgrass Farms in August 1998 and selected the birds to be shipped to Drowns and Lee. When the birds arrived, they so impressed both of the breeders that an arrangement was then made to purchase the remainder of the flock. With this larger number of birds to work with, a network of ten additional small flocks has been established. Through the course of the project, the birds gained the name "Sweetgrass" turkeys to distinguish them from other strains and varieties.

ALBC was very fortunate to have Glenn Drowns and Andy Lee as partners in this project. Mr. Drowns has been active in the conservation of rare turkeys for a long time and has the most extensive collection of rare turkeys in the United States. Not only does he have experience in the management and selection of rare turkey varieties, his hatchery business will provide an avenue to distribute Sweetgrass turkeys to other breeders in the future. Andy Lee, author of *Chicken Tractor: The Gardener's Guide to Happy Hens and Healthy Soil*, is a well-known advocate of sustainable agriculture. He is currently researching management, processing, and marketing options for free-range turkey production and will be evaluating Sweetgrass turkeys in a pasture-based system.

The Sweetgrass turkeys have exceeded expectations for both Andy Lee and Glenn Drowns. Both feel that this strain has immediate and obvious commercial potential. The turkeys are large, vigorous, well conformed, and appear to have a calmer disposition than many others. The color is unusual and may represent a new variant. Alternatively, the birds may carry the rare allele for the grey pattern. Though the mechanism which may link color with conformation and other characteristics is not understood, there may well be a connection that can explain the unusual combination of traits found in the Sweetgrass strain.

It will be some time before we know the contribution Sweetgrass turkeys will make to the genetic conservation of the species or to sustainable turkey production. There is much work to do – breeding, documenting performance, and promoting the turkeys – to ensure the survival of this strain. But a beginning has been made.

If you are interested in participating in the Sweetgrass turkey conservation project, consult Glenn Drowns, Sand Hill Preservation Center, 1878 230 Street, Calamus, Iowa 52729, or Andy Lee, Good Earth Farm, 1702 Mountain View Road, Buena Vista, VA 24416. 🦃

Other varieties and colors

Over the past two centuries, a wide range of varieties, strains, and types of turkeys have been used across the United States. Only nine varieties have historically been recognized by the American Poultry Association, and these have been described above. Many of the non-recognized varieties could be considered "landraces," meaning that they were primarily locally-adapted populations lacking formal standards or written history. This is an obstacle to their evaluation and conservation today.

An overview of historic turkey diversity by Craig Russell (1991, 1998) includes many of the named varieties associated with specific colors. Among those discussed are the Auburn, Black-winged Bronze, Brown, Chestnut, Chocolate, Cinnamon and Spotted Cinnamon, Clay and Claybank, Copper, Gray, Nutmeg, Silver Auburn, Nebraskan, Royal Nebraskan, and Spotted Nebraskan. Comments on a few will give the reader an idea of how this diversity is expressed.

The **Auburn**, or Light Brown, is similar in pattern to the Bronze but the bronze color is replaced by reddish brown. The barring in the flight feathers is reddish brown and white. The **Silver Auburn** is a much lighter version of the Auburn color resulting from the presence of the gene for the Narragansett pattern.

The **Black-winged Bronze or Crimson Dawn** is another variation of the Bronze pattern, with the barring on the flight feathers replaced by with solid black. The result is an attractive bronze bird with generally black wings. Some have white shoulders leading to the peculiar situation where "White-winged Bronze" and "Black-winged Bronze" actually denote the same variety.

Clay, Claybank, and Fawn are darker brown or tan versions of the Buff variety. The **Chocolate**, a uniform chocolate brown throughout, is a much darker fawn or clay. **Cinnamon** and **Spotted Cinnamon** turkeys are much like the Bourbon Red but a slightly lighter shade of red. These varieties were historically found in the South.

Grey turkeys are white with black barring, except for the flight feathers, which have

The Auburn is also known as the Light Brown. Photo by Phillip Sponenberg.

47

The Lilac turkey is a variation on the Slate. Photo by Phillip Sponenberg.

a smearing of black throughout instead of the usual black and white bars. The tail feathers are white with brown or black pigmentation, with a black bar at the end and then a final edging of white. This color variety is close to extinction.

The **Nebraskan** or **Spotted Nebraskan** was introduced in 1947 by R. H. Jandebeur of North Platte, Nebraska, based on a color mutation that appeared in his flock of Broad-breasted Bronze. The term "spotted" is used because the birds are nearly white but have black flecking over the shoulders and on the breast. The white under feathers were an advantage for this variety, as was their broad-breasted conformation. They were popular commercially for a time but are now quite rare.

The **Nittany** turkey was developed at Pennsylvania State University in the 1930s by researchers wanting to produce a new strain of domesticated wild turkeys. The goal was to develop birds similar to wild stocks in size and color pattern but with a more docile temperament, better egg production, and more efficient growth rate. Proposed weights were twenty pounds for mature toms and twelve pounds for mature hens. Though the work was considered successful in that the turkeys were adaptable to retail trade, the Nittany was never produced in large numbers. One of us (R.O. Hawes) saw a small flock in the early 1960s being kept at the home of the superintendent of the Penn State Poultry Farm. Small numbers of birds from this flock were released annually back to the wild. No birds are presently known of this variety, although it may well have contributed to the domestic population of Eastern Wild turkeys.

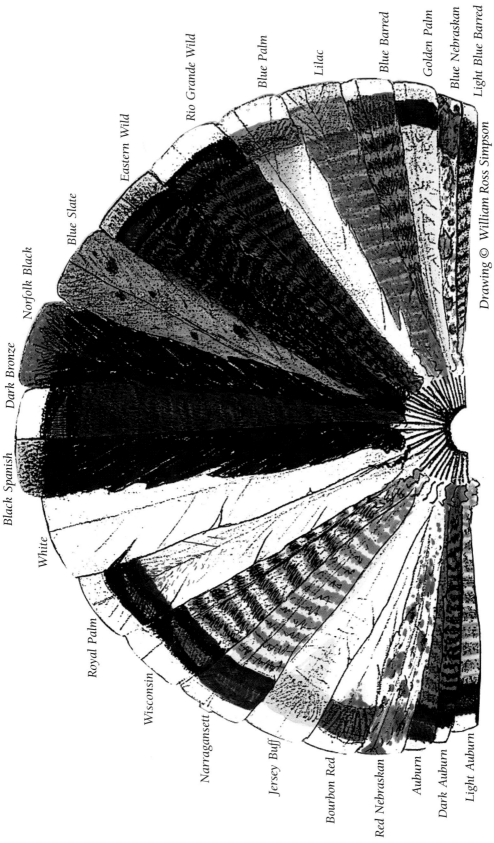

Eastern Wild

Rio Grande Wild

Blue Palm

Lilac

Blue Barred

Golden Palm

Blue Nebraskan

Light Blue Barred

Blue Slate

Norfolk Black

Dark Bronze

Black Spanish

White

Royal Palm

Wisconsin

Narragansett

Jersey Buff

Bourbon Red

Red Nebraskan

Auburn

Dark Auburn

Light Auburn

Drawing © William Ross Simpson

Turkey Tail Feathers

Basic Turkey Color Genetics

By D. Phillip Sponenberg

The basics of turkey color genetics are of interest to breeders who want to conserve color diversity or understand the relationships of turkey colors and varieties. Control of color can be understood throug the concept of a series of sites or "loci." At each site there is a switch with one, two, or occasionally three options, or "alleles." The final color of a bird depends on the sum of alleles at all of the sites.

Genes in birds (and animals) occur in pairs. Each bird gets one gene from its sire and one from its dam. In turn, when the bird reproduces, it passes along one of each pair to its offspring. This means that there are several ways that genes interact. For example, a dominant gene for color can mask a recessive gene when they are paired up at a site. A bird with one dominant gene and one recessive gene will show only the dominant gene but can still pass along the recessive gene to its offspring. In this way, recessive colors can pop up as surprises when two "carrier" birds mate. Surprises can also be caused by genes which are located on the sex chromosomes. Such "sex-linked" genes may be transmitted differently to male and female offspring so it is possible for traits to skip generations in their expression.

When a mutation occurs at a chromosomal site that controls color, it becomes a new allele available in the population. For example, the allele for Black-winged Bronze is a mutation at the Bronze locus. Mutations such as those described below will often modify or dilute other colors or change the patterns caused by the genes already present in the population.

Phillip Sponenberg, ALBC's Technical Coordinator, is a Professor of Genetics and Pathology at the Virginia-Maryland College of Veterinary Medicine and Virginia Tech in Blacksburg, Virginia.

"Wild type" is a genetic term given to the allele at any site that produces the color and pattern found in wild populations. Often the entire genetic compliment of the original pattern is referred to as the "wild type" pattern. This allele functions to allow expression of some aspect of unmodified base color, in contrast to mutations which modify or dilute the base color. The wild type is often the most common allele at a site, and most color varieties are based around only single mutations from the wild type. For example, the Narragansett variety carries all wild type alleles but one, and this one allele modifies the bronze pattern by preventing the formation of the bronzing pigment.

Loci controlling color

Following is a list of the major sites that control color in turkeys. There are additional modification processes but these are merely fine tuning of the colors described below. Remember that for each site, an individual bird will have two genes (one from each parent). The two genes can be the same, or they can be different, in which case one is dominant and one is recessive. Dominant genes are written as capital letters and recessive genes as lower case letters.

- **Bronze** site: three alleles
1. B = Black. This gene is dominant and causes black throughout all the feathers. It is often incompletely dominant, however, so that birds with two black genes look entirely black, but those with only one black gene and one bronze gene may have occasional bronze feathers. (This is sometimes called having one versus two "doses" of black.)
2. b = Bronze. This is the "wild type," responsible for the color found in several varieties of turkeys, including the Bronze.
3. b^1 = Black-winged Bronze. The usual barring of the bronze primary and secondary feathers is replaced by black. (The pattern produced is also called Crimson Dawn.)

Chocolate turkeys are an even brown throughout the plumage. They were once fairly common in the South. Photo by Phillip Sponenberg.

- **Color** site: three alleles
1. C = Wild type. This is dominant and results in full expression of all other colors. It is present in all varieties except for White and Gray.
2. c^g = Grey. This rare recessive reduces reddish-brown pigment and diffuses black through the flight feathers.
3. c = White. This is the mechanism that creates white birds by masking all other colors; it does not, however, act on the color of the beard. White poults may have some pigment.

- **Dominant Slate** site: two alleles
1. D = Slate. This dominant gene dilutes black pigment to a slaty blue, but it has little effect on reddish pigment and leaves it generally unmodified. This is the basis of most Slate birds. The allele "leaks," however, so that birds may have spots, splashes, or flecks of black in many feathers.
2. d = Wild type. This is recessive and leaves black unchanged.

- **Recessive Slate** site: two alleles
1. Sl = Wild type. This is dominant, leaving other colors unchanged.

2. sl = Recessive slate. This dilutes any other color to a lighter form. Birds homozygous for recessive slate often show some pattern in the feathers. Recessive Slate in combination with Buff produces Lilac, a bird with nearly white flight feathers and unpencilled tail feathers.

- **Brown** site: two alleles, sex-linked
1. E = Wild type. This is dominant, leaving other colors unchanged.
2. e = Brown. This recessive replaces black pigment with chocolate brown. For example, it changes Bronze to Auburn, Narragansett to Silver Auburn, and Black to Chocolate.

- **Red** site: two alleles
1. R = Wild type. This is incompletely dominant. Birds with two wild type genes are Bronze, but birds with only one are bronze-red.
2. r = Red. This is incompletely recessive. Birds with two of these gene are the familiar Bourbon Red pattern with red throughout the feathers, some black tips, and white flight feathers. Bourbon Red birds carry their r/r alleles on a Bronze (b/b) background, while

Buff birds carry their r/r alleles on a Black (B/B) background.

- **Narragansett** site: three alleles, sex-linked
1. N = Wild type. This is dominant, with no change in pattern.
2. n = Narragansett. This is a recessive which changes bronze to the Narragansett pattern.
3. n^al = Imperfect albino. This recessive causes birds to be blind and grow poorly, so it is only of scientific interest.

- **Royal Palm** site: two alleles
1. P = Wild type. This is dominant, with no change in pattern.
2. p = Royal Palm. This recessive gene changes the color to Royal Palm type with pale feathers having dark regions at the tips.

The genetics of this pattern are not clearly understood. Some consider it to result from a combination of Palm and Narragansett mutations. Alternatively, one researcher, Ed Buss, proposes that it results from three mutations: Black-winged Bronze, Grey, and Narragansett.

- **Spotting** site: two alleles
1. Sp = Wild type. This is dominant, producing unspotted pattern
2. sp = Spotted. This recessive gene causes the Nebraska type spotting pattern.

Genetic Formulas for Color Patterns

Most of the genetic formulas for the turkey colors make some intuitive sense. Bronze, for example, has no mutants and is similar to the wild type in color. Black, logically, comes from replacing all color with black throughout the plumage. Some of the other colors are based on combinations of genes. Slate, for example, requires that the bird becomes uniformly black, and then the black pigment

is diluted through either dominant or recessive slate mutation. Chocolate, similarly, results from first making the bird entirely black and then replacing all black with chocolate brown throughout. Buff is a combination of black and red mechanisms. The mechanism for black makes the bird uniformly black and then the mechanism for red essentially removes the black pigment with buff the result.

Many other combinations are possible, and some of them have been generated at various times by crossing different varieties. For example, Royal Palm strains have been developed that replace the black by red, slate blue, or chocolate. The potential combinations are numerous, although few of these have ever been developed as hallmarks of well-known varieties.

If you want to read more about color inheritance, consult articles by Buss (1989) and Savage (1990). Dr. Savage also has a web site showing turkey colors, including some poult colors: <http://osu.orst.edu/dept/animal-sciences/poultry/T67.html#anchor820572>. Roberts (1996) and the Feathersite web site (in the Sources of Information) also have good photographs of turkey color patterns.

Color / Pattern Mutations

The Bronze pattern is regarded as the "wild type" when considering turkey plumage patterns. The genotype for the Bronze pattern would be written as follows:

b/b C/C d/d Sl/Sl E/(E) R/R N/(N) P/P Sp/Sp

Bronze	no mutations
Black	B (Black)
Black-winged Bronze	b¹ (Black-winged bronze)
Grey	c^g (Grey)
White	c (White)
Auburn	e (Brown)
Bourbon Red	r (Red)
Narragansett	n (Narragansett)
Nebraskan	sp (Spotting)
Royal Palm	p + n (Palm plus Narragansett)?
Slate, dominant	B (Black) + D (Slate)
Slate, recessive	B (Black) + sl (Recessive Slate)
Chocolate	B (Black) + e (Brown)

Chapter 5

Conservation and Use
of Turkey Diversity

"Other than ignorance and neglect, there is no reason to allow the genetic diversity of one of the major meat sources of the world to degenerate. In the past, market trends have allowed genetic resources to disappear, and this could have devastating consequences."

—Paula Johnson (1998a)

THE CONSERVATION OF TURKEY GENETIC DIVERSITY – especially in the form of rare varieties – is urgently needed. What does it take to accomplish this goal? Many contributions are needed. First, rare varieties should be bred and managed as genetic resources. This involves the establishment of networks of breeders working together to select for type and soundness in these stocks. Second, a greater diversity of turkeys should be used in agriculture, especially in diversified, sustainable agriculture where birds are expected to thrive on range. This includes evaluating the performance of different varieties so that the best genetic resources for each niche can be chosen. Third, turkeys should be exhibited in a number of different settings in order to introduce them to a wider audience of hobbyists and fanciers. Finally, the research strains of all kinds, including Large Whites, may be of great genetic importance and their conservation should be supported by universities and the turkey industry. Using a diverse array of strategies is the only way that turkey diversity can be protected for the future.

Conservation breeding of
rare varieties

Conservation breeding is the management of individual flocks of turkeys (or other birds and animals) as genetic resources for their breed or variety. The following discussion is adapted from *A Conservation Breeding Handbook* by D. P. Sponenberg and C. J. Christman (1995). There are five elements of conservation breeding:

1. A knowledge of the history and characteristics of the breed (or variety), including its production parameters. This can be thought of as the breed's "genetic heritage."

2. An evaluation of the numerical and genetic status of the breed to determine its needs, both in terms of population and genetic diversity. Distinct bloodlines or historic types often represent genetic resources within the population and deserve special attention.

3. A determination of how individual flocks may serve the long-term needs of the variety. Flock cans be selected for slightly different purposes but all can be complementary.

4. The design of a breeding program which incorporates (a) the selection for breed type, soundness, and production, and to improve these qualities as possible; (b) the use of several sires to maintain genetic variation in each generation; and (c) the control of inbreeding so that it does not affect the entire flock.

5. A periodic re-evaluation of the status of the breed, as well as the flock, and revision of the breeding program as needed.

The application of these elements to a rare turkey variety depends upon its current status. For example, selection of breeding stock is necessary, but culling may be limited in the most critically rare populations in order to maintain maximum genetic diversity. As the population increases, selection for soundness can be initiated. Selection for type, including performance characteristics, is used as soon as possible to improve the consistency and performance of each generation.

Conservation of turkeys and other poultry works best when a rare variety is divided among a network of several flocks. Networks offer several advantages. They protect against the sudden loss of an entire population to predators or disease, as well as more insidious losses from poorly-considered selection programs. A larger number of small flocks will keep more males, and thus more genetic range is available to counter the effects of inbreeding. A bonus is the fact that each flock owner will be making slightly different management and selection decisions, and this means the variety is adapting to several different settings.

There is no single recipe for conservation breeding which used in every flock to guarantee that genetic diversity is protected. Nor is such a recipe necessary. The goal is not uniformity of birds or breeders. By understanding the basic principles and methods of conservation breeding and by using selection appropriate to their birds, however, individuals can develop effective programs to fit their own stock and capabilities. A diversity of well-considered approaches within the conservation philosophy is healthy for a breed and its stewards.

Turkeys must be used in a variety of niches for the full genetic diversity of the species to be conserved. These are Wishard Bronze turkeys, quite at home on Montana range. Photo courtesy of Ray Suiter.

Successful incubation and hatching are essential for turkey conservation.
Photo courtesy of USDA-APHIS.

Breeding protocols

The simplest breeding plan consists of the periodic swapping of toms among breeders. It is not necessary to exchange birds annually; every two or three years is sufficient. What is important is that all flocks produce birds to exchange, rather than a single flock supplying the rest of the group.

A more complicated version calls for the maintenance of three or more distinct breeding groups or pens within each turkey flock or within a network. Every breeding season (or every other breeding season), the males are rotated to the next group of females in a circular pattern. For example, the daughters produced by group A remain in that group, and the males are moved to group B, where they will be mated with the B daughters. The daughters from pen C remain in group C, but the sons are moved to group A.

The goal is to minimize the effects of inbreeding. The number of males used for breeding is more critical than the total number of birds in the population. For example, twelve to fifteen females and three toms divided among three breeding pens is far better in terms of maintaining genetic diversity than twenty-five hens and one tom. This is the concept of effective population size.

For larger flocks and larger spaces, breeders may want to consider a multiple-sire mating program, whereby the males are divided into three stable, separate groups. (The stability of the groups is necessary to avoid fighting.) The females are kept in a single flock, and the groups of males are rotated sequentially through the flock of females. Success depends on having enough space so that all of the males have the opportunity to mate. By rotating the males, we allow a greater number of males to take part in the mating than if we had left the flock permanently mated for the season with only one group of males. It is also possible to pedigree the poults from each group of the males, though this requires a long wait between male groups. Female turkeys have a very efficient semen storage capability, and they have been known to be fertile up to eight weeks after removal of the males. Using this system, two shifts of males (and resulting hatches) could be made in any one season.

Many other breeding protocols are available. For example, older poultry books such as *Turkey Management* by Marsden and Martin

55

Turkeys are alert and active foragers, and if given good range they can find much of their own food. These are Broad-breasted Bronze turkeys. Photo courtesy of the Department of Animal and Veterinary Science, University of Maine.

(1939, 1955), have excellent suggestions for selection of stock with emphasis on improvement of production. Other breeders may also have developed protocols based on their own experiences.

A form of "grading-up" as used in livestock may be applicable when the goal is to rescue the very rarest varieties. This is a way to increase the number of females in the population through a limited outcross to the Bronze variety. A male of the rare variety is mated to Bronze hens. The female offspring are then mated back to a different male of the original variety. The female offspring of that cross are genetically three-quarters of the original variety, and they may be the appropriate color by now as well. They are mated back to a male of the original variety, producing poults which are seven-eighths the original variety. These poults should be selected according to the standard for the variety, and the conforming individuals used for breeding. Though the rescue is essentially complete, it may take additional selection to completely recapture original type. The population has not only increased in number, but genetic breadth has also been added to improve vigor.

For more information on conservation breeding, contact the American Livestock Breeds Conservancy, listed in the Sources of Information section at the end of this book.

Turkeys in sustainable agriculture

Conservation breeding by a core group of stewards is essential to saving rare turkeys from extinction. At the same time, it is also necessary to recruit new people to become supporters of each rare variety. Farmers can be an important part of this network. As Cary Fowler and Pat Mooney (1990) wrote, "Agricultural diversity will not be saved unless it is used. The value of diversity is in its use. Only in use can diversity be appreciated enough to be saved. And only in being used can it continue to evolve, thus retaining its value."

Rare varieties of turkeys have clear potential use in sustainable agriculture. Having not undergone generations of selection for intensive husbandry, these varieties retain the ability to forage actively for insects, larvae, seeds, nuts, plants, and other foods. They can often find a good portion of their diet while providing valuable biological pest control in crop or pasture settings. Anecdotal reports stress the hardiness and disease resistance of rare varieties, and this may be of interest to farmers producing for specialty meat niches. Also, rare varieties may retain the maternal ability necessary for females to hatch and raise their own young.

There are some obvious challenges in using rare varieties that should be acknowledged, however. There has been practically no data collected on the production qualities of these varieties for a half-century. It is likely that production potential has declined due to small population sizes and reduced selection. Of course, we know that no turkeys can compete with the Large White in an intensively managed, high-input system when rapid growth rate, feed efficiency based on grain, quantity of meat yield, and rate of egg production are measured. Some rare varieties may not have the production levels necessary to be a viable choice for even a small-scale producer. The more general obstacles to the production of free-range turkey (such as local access to processing facilities and marketing outlets) should also be addressed early on.

Despite the challenges, interest in "free range" turkey production is soaring among practitioners of sustainable agriculture. Will rare varieties be able to take advantage of this expanding niche? We don't know. Most farmers use the Large White because it is the most common variety. Though the difficulties with raising such turkeys on range have been widely documented (e.g. Cramer 1993), there has been almost no discussion of the alternative genetics that rare varieties have to offer.

Herman Beck-Chenowith of Creola, Ohio, is one of the few agriculture writers to consider this topic. His *Free-range Poultry Production and Marketing* manual (1996) calls for farmers to evaluate the genetic diversity available in the form of poultry breeds, varieties, and strains in order to find the best birds for their production niche. Beck-Chenowith also points out that almost all farmers producing poultry, whether turkeys or other species, rely on the annual purchase of birds from a hatchery. This saves the trouble and expense of keeping breeding stock, but it also means that producers have no ability to determine what types of birds they will be able to purchase from year to year. Given the business pressures facing hatcheries, it is also risky, since desirable strains could be lost without notice. Instead, farmers (as individuals or as groups) should begin to take more initiative and responsibility in establishing sources of turkeys that will be selected for health and productivity on range.

The choice of varieties for sustainable production should be based on a clear understanding of the jobs the turkeys are expected to do and the environment in which they'll be

Turkeys may be housed in small, portable houses such as this "turkey tractor." Photo by Carolyn Christman.

raised. For example, what quality and quantity of range is available? Will foraging be integrated with the grazing of other animals or the production of crops? What type of fencing and housing will be used? What time(s) of year will turkeys be sold, and how long should it take for them to reach market weight? How will they be processed and marketed? Must the birds have light under-feathers or can the presence of some pigmented pinfeathers be used to marketing advantage by demonstrating that these are, indeed, an alternative to supermarket turkeys? It may take several seasons to evaluate different varieties, strains, and types of turkeys, but the time spent will be well invested. The use of networks would be beneficial by allowing for on-farm research to proceed at different sites and for stocks to be shared.

Research should also evaluate selection strategies for improving production characteristics in purebred varieties. It would be useful to test the results of crossing varieties, either rare varieties to each other or rare varieties with medium white type females. When two unrelated parent lines are bred together, hybrid vigor results and may improve survival and production qualities in the offspring. The greatest benefit would come from a three-way cross, that is, if the crossbred female is kept for the second generation and bred back to a pure line male. As long as the purebred parent varieties are maintained, crossbreeding would support conservation breeding. The idea needs a champion who will try a few crosses and report back on the results.

Though interest in sustainable turkey production is high, there is relatively little information in print about this topic. Books on poultry written in the first half of the 1900s (when turkeys were raised on range) are the best reference materials. Many of the books in the Bibliography are good resources for beginning turkey farmers. The Sources of Informa-

tion list in the back of this book includes several organizations which can also provide information about turkey husbandry and production.

Exhibition and promotion

Because of their size, space requirements, and feed consumption, the keeping of turkeys for purely exhibition purposes has declined alarmingly since the decades of the 1930s and 1940s. Good exhibitions of turkeys are few and far between. For example, the Ohio National Poultry Show in 1998 included 44 turkeys. Compare that figure with the 7,044 bantam chickens, 3,366 standard chickens, and 1,884 waterfowl entered at the same show.

Interest in exhibiting turkeys may be increasing, however. There were 48 turkeys at the Kansas Classic show, held in Hutchinson, Kansas, in November 1998. All of the standard varieties were shown, with the exception of the Beltsville White. The turkey breeders present dedicated the show to Norman Kardosh, who has bred and raised turkeys for most of this century and been an inspiration to breeders across the country.

Most poultry judges see turkeys infrequently. When they do, they may place too great an emphasis on the commercial traits, primarily breast width. The broad-breasted turkey has become the market standard and, it seems in some cases, the show standard as well. When Large White turkeys are shown as White Hollands and Broad-breasted Bronze as Standard Bronze, it is difficult for judges to ignore these muscular specimens. While the industrial types will continue to be the norm for large scale commercial operations, the standard varieties can perform well in many other production systems, and their qualities should also be recognized in the show ring.

The American Poultry Association *Standard of Perfection* for turkeys should be revised to give proper consideration to those breeders

The Kansas Classic turkey show, held in November 1998, was one of the largest turkey shows in 25 years. Pictured are (left to right): Danny Williamson with best of variety Black hen, Dean Klaus with best of variety Slate hen, Jerry Klaus with Norman Kardosh's best of variety Bourbon Red tom, Norman Kardosh with Reserve Champion Narragansett tom, Frank Reese, Jr., with Grand Champion Stanard Bronze tom, and Jim Adkins, the judge. Photo by Laura Van Horn, courtesy of Frank Reese, Jr.

who are maintaining the Standard Bronze and authentic White Holland. Currently, the White Holland section states that the variety "may be referred to as Broad-breasted White or Large White," and the Bronze section similarly says that this variety is "sometimes referred to in modern commercial technology as Broad-breasted Bronze." The British poultry standard takes a different position by stating: "The standards published here relate solely to the traditional type pedigree breeds of turkeys, which are naturally bred and not related in any way to the modern commercial, broad-breasted types, which are not considered appropriate for the showroom."

We all recognize that the detailed requirements of form and feather set out for exhibition poultry are not always compatible with the simultaneous selection for production of meat and eggs. Nevertheless, many breeders enjoy the challenge of producing perfect exhibition birds. On a more modest level, even simple exhibits of turkeys at a state or county fair can be effective in introducing the traditional varieties to new audiences. This type of breeding can also contribute to the conservation of turkey diversity. Without a change in the APA *Standard,* and judges who are in tune with conservation efforts, however, breeders will not be encouraged to exhibit their turkeys.

A group of turkey breeders are forming a Standard Turkey club to become an advocate for the conservation, exhibition, and use of traditional varieties of turkeys. This idea was first discussed by the Heritage and Rare Turkey Group on the Internet. This group can complement the work of the umbrella organizations, such as the American Livestock Breeds Conservancy, Rare Breeds Canada, and the Society for the Preservation of Poultry Antiquities. There is much work to do in attracting new breeders and providing a way for them to trade information, experiences, and stock.

Maintenance of turkey research stocks, though expensive, is an important investment in conservation. Photo courtesy of USDA-APHIS.

Research stocks

An important but less well-known element of poultry genetic resources are the "research stocks" held by land grant universities across North America. These stocks are generally well-defined, closed genetic populations which have undergone sometimes unique selection pressures over many generations. The knowledge gained from the study of such populations has been critical to modern understanding of genetics, physiology, reproduction, and many other biological processes and species characteristics.

While some of the stocks have been incorporated into the industrial lines, those populations which have remained distinct are of considerable genetic interest. For example, scientists at Ohio State University, one of the very few universities still raising research strains of turkeys, recently published DNA analysis demonstrated that the OSU populations of Large White turkeys were distinct from those used by industry (Ye et. al. 1998). Another example is the population of White Midget turkeys held at the University of Wisconsin, interesting because of their similarity to the Beltsville Small White.

Recently, however, the great majority of university research flocks have been dispersed as a cost-cutting practice often associated with the merger of poultry science and animal science departments. Delany and Pisenti (1998), of the University of California at Davis, write, "The recent elimination of a number of unique avian genetic research stocks and the imperiled status of entire research collections as well as specific lines within relatively stable collections has alarmed biologists who value and utilize such stocks. Unfortunately, despite recommendations by numerous scientists, committees, workshops, and councils, no formal plan exists for the conservation of these poultry genetic resources." The authors have proposed the development of a North American Avian Genetic Resources System (NAAGRS) to inventory, oversee, and encourage the conservation of these populations to guarantee their availability in the future. A formal report, by Pisenti et al., is now in press.

Though rare standard varieties are not being kept as research stocks currently, poultry scientists and small-scale breeders share an interest in documenting and conserving turkey genetic resources. The more broadly-based and diverse our methods of conserving genetic diversity, the more likely we will be to accomplish our goals.

Chapter 6

Conclusion

"People who raise rare turkeys are a rare breed themselves."
—Carolyn Christman

ONLY AS LONG AS PEOPLE ADMIRE and find use for the turkey will the genetic diversity in this magnificent species survive. Although it is now possible to cryopreserve turkey semen and embryos, these techniques are found in only a few laboratories (Delany and Pisenti 1998). As a result, conservation rests on the raising of birds each year by hatcheries, individual breeders, and university researchers. Living flocks across the country must be our gene banks.

The work done by rare turkey breeders benefits all of society. What do the breeders themselves gain? They may reap surprising rewards, such as the satisfaction of protecting something unique and valuable from extinction. There is also the pleasure of working with the birds themselves. Turkeys – especially the old varieties – are curious, colorful, friendly, and entertaining. These qualities are at the core of why people make the commitment to turkey conservation. They cannot bear for such birds to be lost forever.

Can you help?

If you're interested in raising turkeys, the first step is to learn more about turkey husbandry. The Sources of Information list and the Bibliography in the back of this book are good places to begin. Carefully consider your own resources, especially your ability to provide predator-resistant fencing and housing. If you decide to raise turkeys, it's recommended that you find a network of breeders and producers who can help you keep learning as you go. There may be a local network of people you can find through your local Cooperative Extension Service, sustainable agriculture organization, farmers' market, poultry fanciers' group, or agriculture newspapers. Unfortunately, in most parts of the country there are relatively few people who raise rare varieties of turkeys, so your network is more likely to be made up of breeders across the United States or Canada. Such groups can nevertheless work well, even for sharing stock, given the relative ease of shipping poults. Remember to add a membership to ALBC and the other national organizations to your networking resources!

The second step is to choose an appropriate variety – one that you'll enjoy and is at the same time a good fit for your experience level and resources. Generally, the very rarest strains and varieties should be in the hands of more experienced breeders, while novices might start with varieties or strains which are better established. If you want to raise turkeys to sell, either as live birds or as meat, you'll need to investigate the elements of this business enterprise, especially processing and marketing options, as well as local and state regulations.

Experience is the best teacher. Your goals will change as your skills increase, and you may graduate to conservation work with rarer populations. You will also be improving your ability to evaluate your stocks, select for breed type and soundness, and make your own flock a genetic resource for the variety it represents.

As a consumer, you can look for opportunities to purchase free range turkey from local markets and encourage your friends to do the same. By supporting this niche, you increase the possibilities for "alternative" turkey production and may encourage farmers to experiment with rare varieties.

Whether you raise birds or not, you can help spread the word about turkey conservation. Think of how many people you can reach just by purchasing extra copies of this book for donation to your local libraries, high school vocational agriculture departments, Cooperative Extension Service offices, nature centers, zoos, or historic sites.

Conservation of turkey diversity is most likely to succeed if we use a diverse array of strategies and involve many different groups of people. As Fowler and Mooney (1990) have written, "What diversity is saved depends on who is consulted. How much is saved depends upon how many people are involved."

Will you help?

Paula Johnson with a Bourbon Red turkey hen. Photo by Mary Ellen Nicholas.

Why turkeys? I'm in love and it's been 46 years

By Frank R. Reese

My first remembrance of turkeys was over 40 years ago when I was five or six years old. I remember going to the farm north of ours, owned by Verle and Agnes Trow. The Trow family raised about 20,000 Bronze turkeys every year. It was then that I fell in love with turkeys.

I joined the 4-H club when I was eight, and, of course, I had to raise turkeys. My dad took me to the Great Northern Hatchery in Salinas, Kansas, where he bought me 25 Broad-breasted Bronze poults. We would raise them through the spring and summer and butcher them in the fall. My job was to walk with the turkeys out to the pastures and crop fields so that they could eat the grasshoppers and other insects. Turkeys are similar to sheep in that it is easy to walk along and herd them.

When I was eleven, my Jersey Black Giant chickens won at our county fair, and I got to take them to the Kansas State Fair. At the fair, I saw my first Standard Bronze, Black Spanish, Royal Palm, Narragansett, White Holland, and Bourbon Red turkeys. I also met Norman Kardosh, the "turkey man" of the poultry world, who is still my

Frank Reese is pictured holding a Standard Bronze turkey. Photo courtesy of Frank Reese.

friend today. He began to share his vast knowledge of turkeys with this wide-eyed kid, and I realized I wanted to start my own flock. My mother got me a round incubator, and I bought a trio of Standard Bronze poults from Norman. Raising turkeys was harder than I thought, but I persevered.

When I was in high school, I met Sadie Lloyd from Abilene, Kansas. She raised 20,000 Bourbon Red turkeys every year. It was such a beautiful sight to see that many Reds at one time. I bought some Bourbons from Sadie and showed them at our county fair and won. In fact, I eventually beat Norman with those birds, and I still remind him of that today!

I've really learned the importance of selection for soundness in my flock. Today I raise Bronze, Bourbon Red, Black Spanish,

Frank Reese is a member of the American Livestock Breeds Conservancy. He raises Standard Bronze and other rare breeds and varieties of livestock at his Good Shepherd Ranch in Lindsborg, Kansas. This article first appeared in ALBC News 15 (6) November/December 1998.

Narragansett, and Slate turkeys. My birds breed on their own, lay well, and are good mothers. I emphasize the long, straight, and strong legs that are well placed under the turkeys. In the old days, turkeys had great stamina. They were even walked to market. This is a great contrast to the commercially grown birds of today which are short legged and unbalanced. If a bird can't stand, walk, or carry itself, what good is it? I feel you must also check the breast bone (called the keel) to make sure it is straight and without deformities. As Hy Patton (who would be 100 years old if he were alive today) told me, "It doesn't matter how beautiful the bird is. If it doesn't do what it was meant to do, it isn't any good."

After all these years, of all the birds I raise, the Kardosh strain Standard Bronze turkeys are my main love. I select my turkeys according to the 1874 *Standard of Perfection*. It is a real challenge to get the feather patterning of the Bronze right, with good bronzing along with "rainbowing" in the main and secondary tail feathers and white on the tail feathers of the gobblers. It is also a challenge to keep good white lacing on the breast feathers of the hens.

As I grow older, my main concern is what is going to happen to my turkeys. I know of no one else who raises a large number of Standard Bronze. To conserve genetic diversity, there must be several people who keep large numbers of each variety and will share their birds with other breeders.

If you choose to raise turkeys, it's important to talk to some of the people who have raised them for years. There are not many of these people left. I have learned so much from Norman Kardosh, Sadie Lloyd, Agnes Trow, Bill Cawley, Hy Patton,

and a few others. For example, Norman knew all of the breeders of the 1920s and 1930s, and he learned their breeding secrets. That is why whenever Norman comes to Good Shepherd Ranch, I get his help to select my breeding birds for the next year. Norman has raised, shown, and judged turkeys for close to seventy years, and that kind of knowledge is priceless. It must be saved and shared.

I am concerned at some of the things I hear today. It seems that some people are trying to save a color pattern of a turkey variety without being equally concerned about the conformation of the breed. We must be selecting for more than color. The size, health, balance, breeding ability, and egg and meat production must also be on our list of priorities.

Someone once asked me why I love turkeys. In fair truth, I don't know. It seems that this feeling has always been there. Raising turkeys is a lot of work, but it is my labor of love. Unlike the negative stereotype of today, turkeys have so much personality that it is easy to make them into pets. They are so smart that they are into everything and will come into the house if you let them! Keeping young turkeys entertained but out of trouble is fun and can be a challenge.

I hope that some of you will take to raising turkeys and make a commitment to the historic and rare varieties. They can give you enjoyment for a long time. I have a hen that is twelve years old and a gobbler going on to nine years. I'll admit though, that it's hard to be indifferent about turkeys. You either love them or hate them. But if you give turkeys a chance, maybe you too will fall in love.

Bibliography

American Poultry Association. 1998. *The American Standard of Perfection*. Lincoln, Nebraska: Jacob North Publishing Company. (Available from the APA, c/o Lorna Rhodes, 133 Millville St, Mendon, Massachusetts 01756.)

Arrington, Louis. n.d. *Small Turkey Flock Management*. North Central Region Cooperative Extension Publication 60.

Beck-Chenowith, Herman. 1996. *Free-range Poultry Production and Marketing: A Guide to Raising, Processing, and Marketing Premium Quality Chicken, Turkey, and Eggs*. Creola, Ohio: Back Forty Books. (Available from Back Forty Books, 26328 Locust Grove Road, Creola, Ohio 45622.)

Bennett, John C. 1850. *The Poultry Book*. Boston: Phillips, Sampson and Company.

Bixby, Donald E., Carolyn J. Christman, Cynthia J. Ehrman, and D. Phillip Sponenberg. 1994. *Taking Stock: The North American Livestock Census*. Blacksburg, Virginia: McDonald and Woodward Publishing Company. (Available from ALBC, PO Box 477, Pittsboro, NC 27312.)

Buss, Edward G. 1989. "Genetics of Turkeys: Origin and Development," *World's Poultry Science Journal* 45, March.

Christman, Carolyn and Laura Heise. 1987. *AMBC Poultry Census and Soucebook*. Pittsboro: American Minor Breeds Conservancy. (Previous name for American Livestock Breeds Conservancy.)

Cline, L. E. 1929. *Turkey Production*. New York: Orange Judd Publishing Company.

Cramer, Craig. 1993. "Top-Flight Turkeys," *New Farm* 15 (3), March/April.

Crawford, R. D. 1984. "Turkey," in *Evolution of Domesticated Animals*, edited by Ian L. Mason. London: Longman Group Limited.

———— 1990. *Poultry Breeding and Genetics* (editor). Amsterdam: Elsevier.

De Crevecoeur, J. Hector St. John. 1963. *Letters from an American Farmer*. (Originally published 1782.) New York: New American Library/Signet Classics.

Delany, Mary E. and Jacqueline M. Pisenti. 1998. "Conservation of Poultry Genetic Research Resources: Consideration of the Past, Present, and Future," *Poultry and Avian Biology Review* 9 (1); 25-42.

Ensminger, M. E. 1992. *Poultry Science*. (Third Edition.) Animal Agriculture Series. Danville, Illinois: Interstate Publishing Company.

Fowler, Cary and Pat Mooney. 1990. *Shattering: Food, Politics, and the Loss of Genetic Diversity*. Tucson, Arizona: University of Arizona Press.

Freese, Betsy. 1998. "Turkeys get on track," *Successful Farming*, November.

Gascoyne, J. 1989. "Recent Advances in Turkey Science," *Poultry Science Symposium* (21), edited by C. Nixey and T.C. Grey. Butterworth Publications.

Hamilton, S. W. 1951. *Profitable Turkey Management*. (Eighth Edition.) Cayuga, New York: The Beacon Milling Company.

Hawes, Robert O. 1998. "The Perilous State of Turkey Varieties," *The American Livestock Breeds Conservancy News* 15 (1), January/February.

Johnson, Paula. 1998a. "The General History and Conservation Crisis of the Domesticated Turkey." Presentation given at the 1998 Annual Meeting of the American Livestock Breeds Conservancy, June 26-28, Farmington, New Mexico.

——— 1998b. *SPPA Turkey Census Report*. Las Cruces, New Mexico: Society for the Preservation of Poultry Antiquities. (Available for $5 from Paula Johnson, 2442 Mayfield Lane, Las Cruces, New Mexico 88005, (505) 526-3109. Make checks payable to SPPA.)

Jull, Morley A. 1930. "Fowls of Forest and Stream Tamed by Man." *National Geographic* 57 (3), March.

Kennamer, James E. 1995. "Feather Color Oddities in Wild Turkeys," *Turkey Call* September/October.

Kennamer, James E., and Mary C. Kennamer. No date. *Wild Turkey Status and Range*. NWTF Wildlife Bulletin 22. Edgefield, SC: National Wild Turkey Federation.

Kennamer, James E., Mary C. Kennamer, and Ron Brenneman. n.d. *History of the Wild Turkey in North America*. NWTF Wildlife Bulletin 15. Edgefield, South Carolina: National Wild Turkey Federation.

Lamon, Harry M. and Rob R. Slocum. 1924. *Turkey Raising*. New York: Orange Judd Publishing Company.

Mallia, J. G. 1998. "Indigenous domestic turkeys of Oaxaca and Quintana Roo, Mexico," *Animal Genetic Resources Information* 23.

Marsden, Stanley J. 1967. "The Beltsville Small White Turkey," *World's Poultry Science Journal* 23.

——— 1971. *Turkey Production*. Agriculture Handbook 393. Washington, DC: Agriculture Research Service, United States Department of Agriculture.

Marsden, Stanley J. and J. Holmes Martin. 1939 *Turkey Management* (First Edition). Danville, IL: Interstate.

——— 1955 *Turkey Management* (Sixth Edition). Danville, IL: Interstate.

McClintic, Christine. 1995. "Conservation of Another Sort," *The Furrow* 100 (4).

McGinty, Brian. 1978. "The American Turkey," *Early American Life* 9 (5), October.

Mercia, Leonard S. 1981. *Raising Your Own Turkeys*. 1981. Pownal, Vermont: Storey Communications.

Moreng, Robert E. 1995. "Development of the turkey industry in the United States." *Poultry Tribune*, September.

Nabhan, Gary P. 1989. *Enduring Seeds: Native American Agriculture and Wild Plant Conservation*. San Francisco: North Point Press.

National Research Council. 1991. *Microlivestock: Little-known Small Animals with a Promising Economic Future*. Washington, DC: National Academy Press.

Nestor, Karl. 1986. "Turkey Any Time," *Science of Food and Agriculture* 4 (3), September.

Pisenti, J. M., M. E. Delany, R. L. Taylor, Jr., U. K. Abbott, H. Abplanalp, J. A. Arthur, M. R. Bakst, C. Baxter-Jones, J. J. Bitgood, F. Fradley, K. M. Cheng, R. R. Dietert, J. B. Dodgson, A. Donoghue, E. Emsley, R. Etches, R. R. Frahm, A. A. Grunder, R. J. Gerrits, P. F. Goetinck, S. J. Lamont, G. R. Martin, P. E. McGuire, G. P. Moberg, L. J. Pierro, C. O. Qualset, M. Qureshi, F. Schultz, and B.W. Wilson. In press. *Avian Genetic Resources at Risk: An assessment and proposal for conservation of genetic stocks in the USA and Canada. Avian Genetic Resources Task Force Report*. Davis, California: University of California Genetic Resouces Conservation Program, Division of Agriculture and Natural Resources.

Powell, Richard E., Jr. 1990. *Turkey Husbandry in Virginia and the Chesapeake Region 1750–1830*. Colonial Williamsburg Research Report 327. Colonial Williamsburg Foundation Library Microfilm # TR 36. Also published in *Early American History Research Reports from the Colonial Williamsburg Foundation Library* (1992). Alexandria, Virginia: Chadwick-Healey.

Reese, Frank. 1998. "I'm in Love and It's Been 46 Years," *American Livestock Breeds Conservancy News* 15 (6) November/December.

Roberts, Michael, 1996. *Turkeys at Home*. Warwickshire, England: The Domestic Fowl Trust.

Robinson, John H. 1924. *Popular Breeds of Domestic Poultry*. Dayton, Ohio: Reliable Poultry Journal Publishing Company.

Russell, Craig T. 1991. "Old Style Turkeys," *Small Farmers Journal* 15 (1), Winter.

———— 1998. "Turkeys," *Society for the Preservation of Poultry Antiquities Bulletin* 2 (4), Winter.

Schorger, A. W. 1966. *The Wild Turkey: Its History and Domestication*. Norman, Oklahoma: University of Oklahoma Press.

Small, M. C. 1974. "Turkeys" in *American Poultry History 1823–1973*, edited by J.L. Skinner. Madison, Wisconsin: American Publishing and Printing.

Smith, Rod. 1979. "'Young' Turkey Industry Prepares for Market." *Feedstuffs* October 29.

Sponenberg, D. Phillip and Carolyn J. Christman. 1995. *A Conservation Breeding Handbook*. Pittsboro, North Carolina: American Livestock Breeds Conservancy.

Stahmer, Louis A. 1923. "Origin and History of the Turkey." *Poultry Tribune* 29 (4), November.

Sullenberger, David. 1990. "Naturally Mating Bronze Turkey Survives Industry Move to Artificial Insemination," *AMBC News* 8 (1) November/December. (Previous name for *ALBC News*.)

Swaysgood, Susan. 1915. *California Poultry Practice*. San Francisco: Pacific Rural Press.

Taylor, Curtis I., Howard B. Quigley, and Maria J. Gonzalez. n.d. *Ocellated Turkey*. NWTF Wildlife Bulletin 6. Edgefield, South Carolina: National Wild Turkey Federation.

Tyler, Hamilton A. 1979. *Pueblo Birds and Myths*. Norman, Oklahoma: University of Oklahoma Press.

United States Department of Agriculture. 1977. *Turkey Production*. (Reprint Edition.) Garden Grove, California: Marsh Farms Publications.

Watson, George C. 1912. *Farm Poultry: A Popular Sketch of Domestic Fowls for the Farmer and Amateur*. The Rural Science Series. New York: MacMillan and Company.

Weir, Harrison. 1909. *The Poultry Book*, edited by Willis Grant Johnson and George O. Brown. New York: Doubleday, Page and Company.

Williams, Bob. 1997. "North Carolina's big bird has its ups and downs," *News and Observer* (Raleigh, North Carolina), November 26.

Winter, A. R. and E. M. Funk. 1960. *Poultry Science and Practice*. (Fifth Edition). Chicago: J.B. Lippincott.

Ye, X., J. Zhu, S. G. Velleman, and K. E. Nestor. 1998. "Genetic Diversity of Commercial Turkey Breeding Lines as Estimated by DNA Fingerprinting," *Poultry Science* 77: 802-807.

The American Livestock Breeds Conservancy

THE AMERICAN LIVESTOCK BREEDS CONSERVANCY (ALBC) is a national, nonprofit, membership organization protecting genetic diversity in livestock and poultry through conservation of endangered breeds of cattle, chickens, donkeys, ducks, geese, goats, horses, pigs, sheep, and turkeys.

ALBC was founded in 1977 when agricultural historians, seeking livestock for interpretive programs at Old Sturbridge Village and other historic sites in New England, discovered that many of the historically appropriate breeds were nearly extinct. The historians joined with farmers and scientists to form the American Minor Breeds Conservancy (AMBC). The organization moved to Pittsboro, North Carolina, in 1985. The name was changed to the American Livestock Breeds Conservancy in 1993 to reflect the growing threat to all purebred livestock and poultry and a broader conservation focus.

In-house research on breed status and characteristics determines conservation priorities for ALBC. Programs include the operation of a gene bank; bloodtyping and DNA analysis for breed characterization; rescues of threatened populations; and the development of genetic recovery breeding protocols. ALBC educates the public and policy makers about the importance of conserving genetic resources and provides technical support for conservation breeding, registry operation, and livestock use to individuals, breed associations, and agricultural organizations. Recent publications include *Taking Stock: The North American Livestock Census* (1994), *A Conservation Breeding Handbook* (1995), *Noah's Ark Today: Saving Rare Farm Animals from Extinction* (1996); and *A Rare Breeds Album of American Livestock* (1997).

The American Livestock Breeds Conservancy was chartered in Vermont and is a federally designated 501(c)3 nonprofit organization. ALBC is supported by membership dues, gifts from individuals, grants, contracts, and sales of publications and merchandise. You are invited to become a member of the American Livestock Breeds Conservancy and a partner in rare breeds conservation. For information, contact ALBC, PO Box 477, Pittsboro, NC 27312 USA, phone (919) 542-5704, fax (919) 545-0022, e-mail <albc@albc-usa.org>, or web site <www. albc-usa.org>.

About the Authors

Carolyn J. Christman served as Program Co-ordinator for the American Livestock Breeds Conservancy from 1987–1999. A historian, anthropologist, and former high school teacher, she was educated at the University of North Carolina and Wake Forest University. She has authored several publications on rare breeds conservation, including *A Rare Breeds Album of American Livestock*.

Robert O. Hawes is Professor Emeritus of Animal, Veterinary, and Aquatic Sciences at the University of Maine. Dr. Hawes received degrees from the University of Maine, the University of Massachusetts, and the Pennsylvania State University. He has authored several scientific publications, book chapters, and popular articles on poultry production and aquaculture and is currently a member of the Board of Directors of the American Livestock Breeds Conservancy.

Hatchery Sources of Turkeys

As of February 1999

Abendroth Hatchery, W8697 Island Rd, Waterloo, WI 53594, (414) 478-2053
Broad-breasted Bronze, Broad-breasted White*

Cackle Hatchery, PO Box 529, Lebanon, MO 65536, (417) 532-4581
Black Spanish, Blue Slate, Bourbon Red, Broad-breasted Bronze, Broad-breasted White, Royal Palm

Clearview Hatchery, PO Box 399, Gratz, PA 17030, (717) 365-3234
Black Spanish, Blue Slate, Bourbon Red, Wild

Dunlap Hatchery, Box 507, Caldwell, ID 83606-0507, (208) 459-9088
Broad-breasted Bronze, Broad-breasted White

Eagle Nest Hatchery, PO Box 504, Oceola, OH 44860, (419) 562-1993
Broad-breasted Bronze, Broad-breasted White

Grain Belt Hatchery, PO Box 125, Windsor, MO 65360, (816) 647-5522
Broad-breasted Bronze, Broad-breasted White

Harder's Hatchery, Route 101, Box 316, Ritzville, WA 99169, (509) 659-1423
Broad-breasted Bronze, Broad-breasted White

Hoffman Hatchery, Box 128, Gratz, PA 17030, (717) 365-3694
Bourbon Red, Broad-breasted Bronze, Broad-breasted White

Hoover's Hatchery, PO Box 200, Rudd, IA 50471, (800) 247-7014, (515) 395-2730
Broad-breasted Bronze, Broad-breasted White, Wild

Ideal Poultry Breeding Farm, PO Box 591, Cameron, TX 76520-0591, (254) 697-6677
Bourbon Red, Broad-breasted Bronze, Broad-breasted White, Royal Palm, Rio Grande Wild

Inman Hatcheries, PO Box 616, Aberdeen, SD 57402, (605) 225-8122
Bourbon Red, Broad-breasted Bronze, Broad-breasted White, Royal Palm, Wild

Kent Hatchery, RR 3, Box 300, Johnson City, TX 78636, (210) 868-7592
Broad-breasted Bronze, Broad-breasted White

Kruse Hatchery, 1011 CR W 14, Ft. Atkinson, IA 52114, (319) 534-7396
Broad-breasted Bronze, Broad-breasted White

Marti's Hatchery, PO Box 27, Windsor, MO 65360, (660) 647-3156
Broad-breasted Bronze, Broad-breasted White

Mt. Healthy Hatcheries, Inc., 9839 Winton Rd, Mt. Healthy, OH 45231, (800) 451-5603
Broad-breasted Bronze, Broad-breasted White

Murray McMurray Hatchery, PO Box 458, Webster City, IA 50595, (800) 456-3280, (515) 832-3280
Bourbon Red, Broad-breasted Bronze, Broad-breasted White, Wild

Privette's Hatchery, PO Box 176, Portales, NM 88130, (800) 634-4390, (505) 356-6425
Bourbon Red, Broad-breasted Bronze, Broad-breasted White, Royal Palm, Eastern Wild, Rio Grande Wild

Ridgeway Hatcheries, PO Box 306, LaRue, OH 43332, (800) 323-3825, (740) 499-2163
Broad-breasted Bronze, Broad-breasted White

---

*The Broad-breasted Whites available from these hatcheries do not represent the most highly-selected strains held by the turkey industry. Documenting the characteristics and status of these various strains of Broad-breasted White turkeys, while of genetic interest, was not a part of ALBC's research.

Sand Hill Preservation Center, 1878 230th St, Calamus, IA 52729, (319) 246-2299
Beltsville Small White, Black Spanish, Blue Slate, Bourbon Red, Standard Bronze-Wishard strain, Buff, Narragansett, Royal Palm, White Holland, Eastern Wild, and others.

Shank's Hatchery, PO Box 429, Hubbard, OR 97032, (503) 981-7801
Bourbon Red, Broad-breasted Bronze, Broad-breasted White

Stork Hatchery and Farm Store, Box 213, Fredericksburg, IA 50630, (319) 237-5981
Bourbon Red, Broad-breasted Bronze, Broad-breasted White

Stromberg's, PO Box 400, Pine River, MN 56474, (800) 720-1134, (218) 587-2222
Black Spanish, Bourbon Red, Broad-breasted Bronze, Broad-breasted White, Narragansett, Royal Palm

Sun Ray Chicks, PO Box 300, Hazelton, IA 50641, (319) 636-2244
Broad-breasted Bronze, Broad-breasted White

Townline Poultry Farm, PO Box 108, Zeeland, MI 49464-0108, (616) 772-6514
Broad-breasted Bronze, Broad-breasted White

Urch/Turnland Poultry, 2142 NW 47 Ave, Owatonna, MN 55060-1071, (507) 451-6782
Beltsville Small White, Black, Bourbon Red, Standard Bronze, Narragansett, Slate

Wish Poultry, Box 862, Prairie City, OR 97869, (541) 820-3509
Standard Bronze-Wishard strain

Other Sources of Stock

Addresses for individuals raising and selling turkeys can be found through the American Livestock Breeds Conservancy, Rare Breeds Canada, the Society for the Preservation of Poultry Antiquities, and other organizations which appear in the following Sources of Information list.

Sources of Information

American Livestock Breeds Conservancy, PO Box 477, Pittsboro, NC 27312, (919) 542-5704, fax (919) 545-0022, <albc@albc-usa.org>, www. albc-usa.org>. ALBC, the publisher of this book, is a national nonprofit membership organization promoting the conservation of rare turkeys and other farm animals as a way to protect genetic diversity in the livestock species. Contact us for more information, including a membership flyer and catalog of publications. Publications include *A Conservation Breeding Handbook,* with more information about the genetic management of rare varieties of turkeys and other animals. ALBC has also produced *Conserving Rare Poultry Breeds through Flock Evaluation*, a guide for farmers and breeders wanting to document the performance of their birds.

American Pastured Poultry Producers Association, c/o Diane Kauffman, 5207 70th St, Chippewa Falls, WI 54729. APPPA is an organization of people producing or interested in learning about pastured poultry of all species.

American Poultry Association (APA), c/o Lorna Rhodes, Secretary, 133 Millville St, Mendon, MA 01756, (508) 473-8769, <apa@netins.net>, <www. radiopark.com/apa.html> APA promotes the breeding and exhibition of standard poultry and publishes *The American Standard of Perfection.*

ATTRA(Appropriate Technology Transfer to Rural Areas), PO Box 3657, Fayetteville, AR 72792, (800) 346-9140, (501) 346-9140, <www.attra.org>. ATTRA provides producers with information on sustainable agriculture, including poultry production.

The Cooperative Extension Service (sometimes called Agricultural Extension Service) has an office in almost every county in the United States with specialists on many agricultural enterprises, including those with poultry. Consult your county government listings to find the nearest Extension office.

Feathersite web site by Barry Koffler, <www.feathersite.com>. This site features material from the Society for the Preservation of Poultry Antiquities.

Good Earth Farm and Publications, Andy Lee and Patricia Foreman, 1702 Mountain View Rd, Buena Vista, VA 24416, (540) 261-8775. This organization offers on-farm workshop and apprenticeship opportunities. Past publications include *Chicken Tractor: The Gardener's Guide to Happy Hens and Healthy Soil.* Current research priorities include free-range turkey production using Sweetgrass turkeys. A book on the subject, *Turkey Tractor: The Grower's Gobbler Guide,* is planned.

Heritage and Rare Turkey Discussion Group, an electronic mailing list about turkeys, <http:freeyellow.com/members6/rare-heritage-turkey/index.html>. There is no charge to subscribe; go to www.onelist.com or www.onelist.com/subscribe/RareHeritageTurkey or to the address above and click on the membership button. Choose regular mail or "digest" format which groups the messages as one e-mail per day. The group plans to form a Standard turkey club and publish a newsletter called *The Gobbler.* For more information, contact Sheane and Bonnie Meikle, Renasisance Poultry, RR 2, Site 6, Box 7, Ponoka, Alberta, Canada T4J 1R2, <action1@ telusplanet.net>.

National Turkey Federation, 11319 Sunset Hills Rd, Reston, VA 22090, (703) 435-7206, <www. turkeyfed.org>. The Federation is the trade organization representing the turkey industry.

The National Wild Turkey Federation, PO Box 530, Edgefield, SC 29824, (800) 843-6983, (803) 637-3106, <www. nwtf.org>. The NWTF promotes the conservation and management of wild turkeys.

Poultry Press, PO Box 542, Connersville, IN 47331-0542, (765) 827-0932. The *Press* is a leading publication about exhibition poultry.

Rare Breeds Canada, c/o Dr. Tom Hutchinson, Trent University, Program in Environment and Resources Studies, Box 4800, Peterboro, Ontario K9J 7B8, (705) 748-1634, <www.flora. org/rbc>, <rarebreedscanada@trent.ca>. RBC is the Canadian organization working to promote endangered livestock and poultry breeds.

Rare Breeds Survival Trust, attn: Peter King, Field Officer, National Agriculture Centre, Stoneleigh Park, Warwickshire CV8 2LC, England, phone 01144-1203-696-551, fax 01144-1203-696-706. RBST is the British rare breeds conservation organization.

Small Farm Institute / Back Forty Books, c/o Herman Beck-Chenowith, 26328 Locust Grove Road, Creola, OH 45622. The Institute offers on-farm workshops about sustainable poultry production and sells a variety of books, including *Free-range Poultry Production* and *Marketing Premium Quality Chicken, Turkey, and Eggs.*

Society for the Preservation for Poultry Antiquities (SPPA), c/o Glenn Drowns, Secretary, 1878 230th St, Calamus, IA 52729, (319) 246-2299. SPPA was founded to promote historic types and breeds of poultry but is now interested in all aspects of poultry conservation. For a copy of the SPPA Turkey Census Report, send a check for $5 (made out to SPPA) to Paula Johnson, 2442 Mayfield Lane, Las Cruces, NM 88005.

Index